# C.G. JUNG AND THE PROBLEM OF EVIL

## PROBLEM OF EVIL

The Strange Trial of Mr. Hyde

# C.G. JUNG AND THE PROBLEM OF EVIL
## The Strange Trial of Mr. Hyde

John A. Sanford

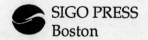

SIGO PRESS
Boston

Synopsis of *The Strange Case of Dr. Jekyll and Mr. Hyde* is from
*Evil: The Shadow Side of Reality* by John A. Sanford, copyright
© 1981, 1991 by John A. Sanford. Reprinted by permission of The Crossroad
Publishing Company.

 SIGO PRESS
25 New Chardon Street, #8748
Boston, Massachusetts 02114

Publisher and General Editor: Sisa Sternback

**Library of Congress Cataloging-in-Publication Data**

Sanford, John A.
    [Strange trial of Mr. Hyde]
    C.G. Jung and the problem of evil : the strange trial of Mr. Hyde
/ John A. Sanford.
        p.      cm.
    Reprint. Originally published: The strange trial of Mr. Hyde. San
Francisco : Harper & Row, c1987.
    Includes bibliographical references and indexes.
    ISBN 0-938434-94-2. -- ISBN 0-938434-93-4 (pbk.)
    1. Good and evil.   2. Man (Christian theology)   3. Jung, C. G.
(Carl Gustav), 1875-1961.   4. Psychoanalysis and religion.
5. Stevenson, Robert Louis. 1850-1894.   Strange case of Dr. Jekyll
and Mr. Hyde.     I. Title.
[BJ1406.S27   1993]
216 -- dc20                                                    90--40064
                                                                  CIP

**Printed in Korea**
∞

*Dedicated to my sister,*
*Virginia T. Clark*

# Contents

# Introduction

We see certain things people do as good and desirable and other things as evil and abhorrent. Those actions we deem good we encourage; those we deem evil we discourage and may even punish as crimes that a decent and ordered society cannot tolerate. Most people manage to live without engaging in conspicuous criminal behavior, but others act in a way that we judge to be outright evil. Evil actions may be individual, such as murder or a rape, or collective, such as the atrocities committed en masse at Dachau and Buchenwald.

Christianity and Judaism have long been concerned with this matter of evil and have tried to find explanations for morally repugnant behavior. The biblical point of view is that the tendency toward evil is deeply ingrained in human nature. Thus the Old Testament says that the human heart is "evil from its infancy" or, as the more picturesque King James translation has it, "the imagination of man's heart is evil from his youth."[1] The Bible says that evil actions constitute sin, which, by definition, means they are actions that go against the will of God. Why human beings should sin is explained in the story of the Fall that took place in the Garden of Eden. Since that time, so the biblical argument goes, human nature has been alienated from God, tends to deviate from God's will, and must be won back to a relationship with God.

However, an explanation such as this does not satisfy the modern mind. Few of us can take the story of the Fall literally today, and attempts to understand the story symbolically and get to its psychological or spiritual truth, while instructive, do not yield any final answer. Nor does the concept of sin appeal to the psychologist, because it shrouds the matter of evil in theological and metaphysical overtones. The fact remains, however, that the psychologist encounters, and is called on to explain, the same evil behavior that confronted the people of the Bible.

It sometimes happens that the most profound statements about problems of life come not from scientists or theologians but from the writers of great literature. One example is Robert Louis Stevenson's novelette *The Strange Case of Dr Jekyll and Mr Hyde*. Stevenson wrote this book in 1886, fourteen years before Freud's *Interpretation of Dreams* and several decades before Jung's psychological works were published. The inspiration for the story, Stevenson tells us, came in a startling dream in which he saw a character who appeared to be benign change into a figure that appeared malevolent. Struck by this, Stevenson made it the central scene in a story of two men who inhabited the same body and personality. The tale so gripped him that he wrote the final version of it in only six days. His characterization of the respectable Dr. Jekyll, who turned into the ugly and deformed Mr. Hyde, has so gripped the collective imagination that virtually every educated person in the Western world knows about Jekyll and Hyde, even those who have not read the story.

All this points to the tale as archetypal, which means that it touches upon universal and profound aspects of our psychology. From the point of view of Jung's psychology, the tale is about the ego and its shadow, that dark and feared part of ourselves that follows us wherever we go and looks all the more sinister the more we try to stand only in the light. So we can understand *The Strange Case of Dr Jekyll and Mr Hyde* as a study in what Stevenson himself called our "tragic and inevitable duality," and thus a monumental study in the origin and nature of human evil.

The psychological importance of Stevenson's novel has been recognized by many people, but only a few have delved into it. The Jungian analyst Barbara Hannah wrote an excellent study of Stevenson's story in her book *Striving Towards Wholeness*.[2] I added a few thoughts of my own in a chapter in my book *Evil: The Shadow Side of Reality*.[3] This present book is one more contribution, a development out of and beyond the ideas that I expressed earlier.

Like Stevenson's original story, this book also originated in what was for me an unusual way. I had no intention of writing anything more on the theme of Jekyll and Hyde. However, in the summer of 1984 I set out by myself on a trip through the mountains and desert of northeastern Nevada. While I was hiking alone through a remote mountain range, there suddenly burst into my mind the idea for the fantasy that follows: an unusual trial of Stevenson's character Edward Hyde in which a defense attorney seeks to defend Hyde against the charges history has made against him. Within the space of a few minues the theme of the story, the characters, the setting, and many of the speeches were clear to me. I could "see" the whole story unfolding like a motion picture. The tale that follows is the direct result of this experience.

Because the book centers around a fantasy, some explanation is in order. Andrew Mapleson, the attorney for the defense, feels strongly that justice has not been done to Edward Hyde. History has judged him to be evil without benefit of a fair trial. Mapleson prevails upon a judge to grant Hyde a hearing *in absentia*, and the story begins. Of course, it partakes of fantasy, since many of the characters in it are contemporary, although others are taken from Stevenson's story. A panel of experts in human affairs and behavior has been appointed by Judge Freeman to offer the court their opinion. Their contributions represent the viewpoints of Jungian psychology, Christianity, the average person, and feminism on the matter of human evil. The appearance of the strange figures from another century enhances the feeling that in the trial the archetypal world intersects with the everyday world of the ego.

The second half of the book is a commentary on the fantasy of the trial. I hope the first half of the book will appeal to the imagination and soul of the reader as well as to the intellect. Many themes are touched upon in the first part of the book; the second part gives the psychological and philosophical background and goes more deeply into Jung's views of the problem of evil. It also gives an opportunity to contrast Jung's views on evil with those of Kunkel and others. In this way many of the viewpoints expressed in the first part of the book are elaborated in the second part. In the study of Jung's view of evil the reader will discover that I do not always agree with the great man from Zurich. The strength of my personal feeling about this deeply important matter may show through on occasion, but I would not want anyone to suppose from this that I do not hold Jung in high regard. Indeed, I probably owe more to him than to any other human being for my understanding of myself. It is only in this one area, evil, that I find myself critical of a man who is, in my view, the greatest psychologist of our time.

A few other comments are in order. It is best if the reader has read Stevenson's original story. For those who have not read it, or need a refresher, there is a summary of the story in the appendix. I recommend that people who have not read Stevenson's original story begin by at least reading the summary. Others will no doubt prefer to go directly to the trial in Part I.

It also should be noted that this is not an attempt to make a complete study of the problem of evil. I discuss the problem mainly as it has surfaced in Western religion and psychology. There is, for instance, very little of the point of view of the East represented in this book; for that, the reader will have to turn elsewhere.

Finally, all the characters in *The Strange Trial of Mr Hyde* are fictional, either characters from Stevenson's story or characters of my own invention. If there is any resemblance to any person, living or dead, it is accidental and unintentional.

NOTES

1. Genesis 8:21. Cf. Jeremiah 7:24; 11:8; 13:10; 16:12; 18:12; 23:17; Proverbs 6:18 ff.; Zechariah 7:10; 8:17.
2. Barbara Hannah, *Striving Towards Wholeness* (Boston: Sigo Press.).
3. John A. Sanford, *Evil: The Shadow Side of Reality* (New York: Crossroad, 1981).

# I  THE TRIAL OF MR HYDE

# 1  The Trial Begins

The courtroom of the Honorable Arthur T. Freeman was as stern, stark, and impersonal as the justice it dispensed. At the rear were two doors through which the onlookers and witnesses entered, wide doors that seemed to symbolize the breadth of a law that included all people. Rows of theater-style folding seats constituted the gallery, where everyone could sit who cared to watch the process of justice at work; this was separated from the inner sanctum of the courtroom by a low railing with a gate in the center. Inside the railing, on the same level as the gallery, two long tables with chairs facing the front were provided for the prosecuting and defending attorneys. To the left of the attorneys' tables as one faced the front of the room was a raised platform with two rows of seats—the jury box. At the front of the room, on a still higher platform, as befitted his high office, was the judge's bench, and off to the side was a small door that led to his private chambers. On another platform, almost as high as the judge's, so all could see it, was the witness stand. The walls of the room were white; a brown carpet provided a trace of color and deadened distracting sounds. Elaborately carved molding around the ceiling, ornate chandeliers, and on one wall a large clock that chimed on the hour gave the room a proper atmosphere of solemnity.

Shortly before 9:00 A.M. on a cold and overcast day the bailiffs opened the doors to the gallery, and a scattering of people soon were seated, the low murmur of their talk rippling through the room. It was a nondescript crowd of various ages, sexes, and colors, but the attention of a careful observer would soon have been drawn to four people whose anxious, intent expressions and antiquated dress distinguished them from the rest.

In the front row of the gallery sat a tall, solemn man of perhaps fifty years of age; a dreary, baggy gray suit with a long, pointed frock coat hung carelessly over his angular frame. His eyes were directed straight ahead, and his face radiated stern, dependable honesty. The man who sat next to him appeared to be the tall man's acquaintance. His well-worn coat and debonair demeanor was that of a man-about-town, although agitated bodily movements betrayed what seemed to be nervousness. Toward the back of the room was an elderly, slightly rotund man with a humble yet genteel bearing, impeccably dressed in an old-fashioned dark suit with a pin stripe and sitting straight as a ramrod with a look on his face of grim determination. All the way in the back, looking as though she desperately wished she were somewhere else, was a plain-looking young woman, clearly a member of what once would have been called the servant class, who could not seem to control her weeping over some matter known, as yet, only to herself.

In the jury box three men and one woman sat stiffly like so many birds perched on a wire. Closest to the judge's bench was a middle-aged man whose manner exuded confident, intelligent self-assurance. Next to him was a tall, dignified older man; the traces of white in his hair added to the impression of a man of distinction. To his right was a younger, middle-aged man whose carefully tailored suit and handsome, confident appearance were those of a successful man-of-the-world accustomed to receiving the well-deserved praise of others. The fourth person was an attractive woman about thirty-five years of age. She was smartly dressed in the manner of a modern woman-of-the-world, but the severe tailoring of her suit could not entirely conceal her graceful feminine curves.

Three men sat at the attorneys' table closest to the jury box. Two were ordinary looking, but the man in the center was impressive: broad, square, and muscular. His physical bearing and obvious energy proclaimed that here was an aggressive attorney, used to winning his cases and not reluctant to intimidate his opponents. The three men were talking together in hushed voices and shuffling papers about. At the other table, sitting alone, was a tall, lanky man of early middle age with slightly graying hair. He appeared to be tired, and exuded none of the confidence of his adversary across the way, but he also seemed a determined man, one who would not give up a fight easily.

The door to the judge's private chambers suddenly opened, and, preceded by a clerk, the Honorable Arthur T. Freeman entered the room. Judge Freeman was a well-built older man who walked with the firm steps of someone used to authority. His confident bearing and penetrating eyes revealed a man who trusted his powers of discernment and knowledge of the law, a man not to be trifled with, who placed the pursuit of justice above all personal, petty considerations. Judge Freeman had an impeccable reputation that transcended the boundaries of his courtroom, and as he entered everyone in the room rose, and the murmur of talk floated away into silence. The clerk took a seat near the bench as Judge Freeman took up his gavel and rapped as a signal that proceedings were now to begin. The people took their seats again, all eyes riveted on the Judge, who remained standing until, when all were dutifully attendant, he spoke.

"Lady and gentlemen," he began, nodding toward the four people in the jury box, "gentlemen of the bar, and men and women in this courtroom who, out of concern for humanity and interest in justice, have chosen to attend this hearing, ours is a most unusual task. Indeed, in undertaking it in this year of our Lord 1987, we depart from all custom and venture into a matter for which there is no precedent: the trial of a person who exists purely as a product of the human imagination. For we are here to determine the guilt or innocence of a man whom some say cannot be tried at all because he never existed, save in the pages of a book, and who, even as a character in fiction, is long deceased. Is it proper, or even possible, to assay the guilt of such a person? Yet it has also been argued that notable characters from the world of fiction have an existence and reality all their own and that, even though they may die in the

pages of a book, they live on in the human imagination. Because of the unusual circumstances it is important that we all
understand the reason we are gathered here today and the nature of our task. A certain party of persons, represented here by
Counselor Andrew Mapleson," the Judge glanced at the tall,
lanky man seated at the attorney's table to his left, "have
claimed that an injustice has been done to a man known as Edward Hyde, whose story is told in a document called *The
Strange Case of Dr Jekyll and Mr Hyde*, which is no doubt at least
generally familiar to all of you. Mr. Mapleson has pointed out
that this man has been condemned as a wanton murderer, nay
more, has been vilified as the very embodiment of all that is
evil in human nature, but that this judgment has been passed
on him without benefit of trial. Mr. Mapleson has argued that,
even though this character is fictional, he still has a certain
kind of existence, and therefore when such a sweeping and de-
famatory judgment is passed on him he deserves a fair hearing.
He has further argued that it is an affront to our system of justice, which states clearly that everyone is innocent until proved
guilty, that such a hearing has not been held and has pointed
out that, no matter how heinous the crime, a person is entitled
to legal representation, which he has offered to provide.

"I cannot say that I agree entirely with this argument. Can
we say that fictional characters have an existence of their own?
Even if we grant that point, can we agree that they have the
same legal rights as those of us whose earthly existence is certi-
fied by our possession of bodies of flesh and blood? Yet to en-
sure that there is no miscarriage of justice I have consented to
grant Hyde an informal hearing, and to allow Mr. Mapleson to
be attorney for the defense. Let no one say that this Court ever
shirked its duty! It will therefore be my purpose and function
to first hear all sides and arguments and then to render a decision that will either exonerate Edward Hyde of the blame
thrust upon him by history's general consensus or will substantiate the well-nigh universal judgment against him.

"When I agreed to undertake this hearing it never occurred

to me that there would be public interest in such an unlikely proceeding. But I can see that a sizable number of you, motivated apparently by an unusually keen interest in justice, or perhaps only by curiosity, are scattered throughout the gallery. You are welcome in this courtroom, and because this is an informal hearing, of an irregular sort, to be conducted along irregular lines, I will briefly introduce to all concerned the participants in our deliberations.

"Mr. Mapleson I have already mentioned; he will represent the defendant, Edward Hyde, *in absentia*, since Mr. Hyde perished by his own hand. The prosecution will be undertaken by the worthy District Attorney Ralph M. Dorset, with his two able assistants, seated at the attorney's table to my right. In the jury box are four persons who will be acting as advisers to the bench. I stress that they are not a jury, that the final decision is in my hands alone, but they are here to offer me advice and counsel, each from his or her own unique professional perspective. Seated immediately to my right," he nodded to the intelligent, confident-looking man, "is the noted psychologist and analyst, Dr. Albert Savant, whose knowledge of unconscious as well as conscious dimensions of personality may well prove crucial in the final determination of this case. Seated next to him," he glanced at the tall man with the white hair, "is the learned Reverend Dr. Albert Christiansen, pastor and theologian of note, who can be counted upon to bring to bear on our deliberations such matters as are known of the divine will. To his right," looking now at the man in the tailored suit, "is Mr. Emory Weatherford, industrialist, philanthropist, and community leader, a man well-suited to speak for all that is eminent and respectable in the life of a decent society. And finally, to his right is the noted family counselor and, may it also be said, charming representative of her sex, Ms. Melanie Wood, who will bring to bear on our deliberations considerations that may well have escaped the attention of the male members of this advisory panel."

Having concluded his talk with these warm remarks about

Ms. Wood, who cringed noticeably under their impact, Judge Freeman paused for a moment. Then he continued, "We are almost ready to begin, but before we do so a word is in order to the attorney for the defense, Mr. Mapleson. Mr. Mapleson," the lanky man stood as his name was called, "before we proceed I must ask you to examine your conscience. You are, I assume, aware of the evil reputation of this Edward Hyde?"

"I am, Your Honor."

"I must urge you, then, not to toy with this Court, nor make a mockery of justice, nor needlessly use up the time of these able men and this woman," the Judge nodded to the people in the jury box, "with an idle cause. You are the one who brought before the attention of the Court the fact that Mr. Edward Hyde has not had a trial. Out of its concern for justice the Court has granted this hearing. Yet it must be pointed out that the defendant has already been tried after a fashion by the general consensus of the public. If you have no new evidence to present, I must ask you to concede at this time the emptiness of your case, and not dally further with this Court."

Mapleson replied, "Your Honor, I have searched my conscience, and it is because of my conscience that I have asked for this hearing, for which I am deeply grateful. I have, of course, no new evidence, because all the evidence that pertains to this case has already been presented in the document you mentioned, *The Strange Case of Dr Jekyll and Mr Hyde*. However, I believe I have a new interpretation of this evidence that will establish that Edward Hyde, though not entirely innocent, is not solely guilty of and responsible for the heinous crimes charged against him."

A low murmur of disbelief became audible in the courtroom; clearly it was curiosity more than doubt about the justice of the general condemnation of Hyde that had attracted people to the trial. Mapleson resumed his seat. The Judge rapped again for attention. "Then we will proceed. Counselor Dorset, I call on you to state the case for the prosecution."

# 2 The Case for the Prosecution

District Attorney Ralph M. Dorset, a veteran prosecutor, rose and moved toward the witness stand. Dorset's confident strength and cunning intelligence, along with a quality of ruthlessness, suited him well for the professional functions he was called upon to perform. His powerful body housed an equally powerful mind; he was a man to inspire fear in all but the most seasoned opponents. The swiftness with which he moved suggested that he regarded the defendant in this case as particularly easy prey; though he might dally with him for a while, the way a cat plays with a mouse before destroying it, the outcome was certain.

"Your Honor," Dorset began, speaking to the Judge but in a voice loud enough to carry to everyone in the courtroom, "it will be my purpose to establish beyond any reasonable doubt, on the basis of the evidence, that the defendant, Edward Hyde, committed horrible and grievous crimes and, notwithstanding the defense of my worthy colleague and adversary Mr. Mapleson, merits the universal condemnation of all well-intentioned members of society. It happens that in this case we have witnesses who observed directly the evil done by Hyde. I propose to call on them to give their testimony and then demonstrate, on the basis of the facts they have brought forward, that the defendant deserves the judgment against him. The first witness is . . . Mr. Richard Enfield!"

At the sound of his name the debonair man seated in the front row of the gallery rose awkwardly to his feet, made his way to the witness stand, and took his seat. His fingers tapped nervously on the arm of the chair, and his face was that of a man for whom a dreaded moment has arrived and who would be devoutly thankful when it was over.

The clerk swore him in. Prosecutor Dorset spoke soothingly, "Would you please give the court your name?"

"Richard Enfield."

"Mr. Enfield, will you please tell the Court where you were in the early morning hours of January 20, 1886?"

"I was coming home through London."

"Were you alone?"

"Yes, I was alone."

"Since it was early morning it must have been dark. Could you see?"

"The night was clear. The streets were stark and empty as a church, but they were well lighted by the street lamps."

"And did you see anything that night, Mr. Enfield, that was out of the ordinary?"

"Out of the ordinary? Oh, indeed it was. It was horrible. I hope I never see anything like it again." And it looked as though Mr. Enfield might burst into tears.

Dorset tactfully waited a few moments for Enfield to regain control of himself—and so the full effect of this display of emotion could be felt by the onlookers. Dorset's voice dripped with sympathy, "I know this must be very difficult for you, Mr. Enfield, but would you please tell the Court exactly what you saw."

"I saw two figures. One was a small man stumping along rapidly in a determined way through the empty street. The other was a little girl of perhaps eight years of age coming from a cross street, also walking rapidly and seeming to be upset about something."

"Then she was proceeding at right angles to the man?"

"That is so."

"Did you think at the time that the little girl was in any danger?"

"No. I thought that they would meet at the corner, and that the man would stop and let the little girl pass by."

"What did in fact happen?"

"Well, sir, the two of them did meet at the corner, but the

man did not stop. In fact he didn't even slow up, but ran right into the little girl, knocking her to the ground . . . "

"And then, Mr. Enfield, what happened then?"

"Well, then . . . then . . . he walked right over her, on top of her, in fact, trampling her body like some damned juggernaut! I tell you, it was hellish to see! He was not like a man but like some kind of devil. Then he continued on his way as if nothing had happened, leaving the terrified child screaming on the ground."

Dorset waited a full sixty seconds to let the full effect of this dramatic and damaging testimony sink in. "What did you do then?"

"Well, sir, I am not ordinarily a brave man, but the horror of this deed was so great that I was aroused to fury and forgot my fear. I took to my heels and chased the man down, and brought him forcibly back to where the child still lay crying on the ground. By now her cries and screams had wakened the neighbors, and quite a group of people had gathered around her. Among them were members of her family—it seems one of them was ill and the little girl had been sent for the doctor."

"What about the man whom you had collared?"

"Well, you would think he would at least look sorry for what he had done, but he showed no shame. He was cool as ice, and he only gave me a look so ugly that I broke into a sweat, chilly though the night was."

"How did the people around the child react to this man?"

"Loathing. You could feel the hate coming out of them. The men were so full of righteous indignation that it looked as though they might strike him. But the greatest reaction came from the women. I tell you they were like harpies, wild with rage, and it was all the cooler heads among us could do to keep them from tearing him to pieces on the spot."

"The child—was she hurt?"

"Fortunately, more frightened than anything else, though no thanks to her assailant. We knew because the doctor for whom the little girl had been sent, wakened like the rest by the noise, came to investigate. First he checked the child over and pronounced her all right, then he looked at the ugly little man who had trampled on her. Now this doctor, a cut-and-dried apothecary if I ever saw one, was not the kind of man you would expect to be emotional, but I tell you that when he looked at my prisoner he turned sick and pale with anger."

"Mr. Enfield, can you tell us the name of this man you captured?"

"I can, sir. His name was Edward Hyde."

"And what did you do after you caught the man?"

"Well we were all horrified. We were all so full of hate, as I have said, that we wanted to kill him, but, that being out of the question, we did the next best thing: we demanded that he make reparations to the girl and her family. This we did not only to make amends to the girl for her painful experience but to find some way to punish him and make him pay for his evil deed. He protested, but since we would not release him until he agreed he was at last compelled to accept our terms. However, since he had little money on him, he asked leave to enter a house nearby where he said he could get the money we required. He returned soon enough with a check signed Henry Jekyll. The check and signature proved genuine, for we detained the man with us until morning and compelled him to go to the bank with us and cash the check."

Dorset again waxed sympathetic. "Thank you, Mr. Enfield. I know it has been difficult for you to remember and tell us about this dreadful experience. Your Honor, this concludes my questions of this witness."

The room was silent until Dorset resumed his seat, whispered a few words to his colleagues, and settled back in his chair. Judge Freeman spoke, "Counselor Mapleson, you have heard the testimony of the witness. You now have the right to cross-examine him." The Judge settled back in his chair expectantly.

Mapleson stood but made no move toward the witness stand. His lanky body seemed weary somehow, like that of a boxer who early in the battle shows his fatigue. "Mr. Enfield," he said quietly, "will you please tell the Court whose house it was that Mr. Hyde entered to get the check?"

"Well, sir, the house belonged to Dr. Henry Jekyll."

"Thank you, Mr. Enfield. I have no further questions, Your Honor."

Judge Freeman looked surprised. Enfield, shaken, but obviously relieved that his ordeal was over, returned to his seat next to the honest-looking man in the baggy gray frock coat. Dorset shot a quick glance at Mapleson that seemed to say, "No questions? What is it you are up to?" But soon his confidence returned. "My next witness, Your Honor, is Miss Sally Jones."

At the sound of her name the plain young woman seated at the back of the gallery wiped her eyes, stood, and made her way to the witness stand like a lamb going to slaughter. So pitiful was her appearance that Judge Freeman spoke to her in his most fatherly voice as she took her place on the witness stand, "My dear young lady, be assured that you are among friends here, that all you have to do is tell the Court the truth as you know it to be."

Miss Jones allowed herself to be somewhat consoled, and Dorset began his questions. He too tried to be fatherly, yet the careful observer would have detected in his voice a hint of impatience. "Miss Jones, would you kindly tell the Court where you were at about 11:00 P.M. on the night of October 11, 1886?"

"In my house as usual, sir, sitting up and looking out the window."

"Wasn't it rather late for you to be awake?"

"I couldn't sleep. I kept thinking and couldn't sleep. So I sat in my room in the dark just staring outside."

"Was the night clear?"

" 'Deed it was. A fog had been there earlier, but, well, you know how funny the fog is in London, now it's here and now it's gone . . . "

"Yes, of course, the fog—but the fog had gone?"

"Yes, like I just said, the fog had gone."

"Was the street lighted?"

"Oh the street lights were on, but more, there was that beautiful full moon . . . oh, the street was so bright with that moon. It made me think such thoughts . . . "

It began to appear that the weepy young Miss Jones was beginning to enjoy this moment of importance after all. Dorset, clearly impatient now, hurried her along. "Yes, of course. The moon does make people think thoughts. But now, tell us what you saw."

The girl's eyes fell. It looked as though she might burst into tears again. Judge Freeman prodded her, "Please control yourself, Miss Jones, and answer the questions."

"Well . . . Well . . . I seen comin' down the street this pretty old gentleman with white hair, as pretty an old man as you ever would want to see, the kind o' old man makes you want to love him, walkin' along with a sprightly kind of walk, happy-like, reminded me of my grandfather . . . "

Dorset interrupted, "And then what did you see?"

"Well, then I seen this other man comin'. And I knew who he was."

"And who was he, please?"

"He was Mr. Hyde, sir. Surely he was."

"How did you know it was Mr. Hyde?"

"'Cause he used to come to visit my master. Twice. And I seen him there in my master's house. Served tea to them. They had some business or other together. I didn't like him neither."

"And what did Mr. Hyde do when he came near the old gentleman?"

Miss Jones once more had to wipe her eyes. "Well . . . they met. And it seemed like the pretty old man said somethin' nice to Mr. Hyde, like a friendly greetin', maybe, like you might do. But Mr. Hyde didn't say nothin' back. 'Stead he lifted up the heavy cane he was carryin' like he was angry about somethin', and he began to beat that old man with it like a madman."

"How many times did he hit him?"

"Over and over . . . like he'd never stop hittin' him. And the old man fell to the ground. And still he beat him with the cane, until I could hear the old man's bones crack. And then Hyde, he trampled on that old man, jumped on him ape-like till his body fell over into the gutter. And then I don't know what happened 'cause I fainted . . . I couldn't stand no more." And with this recollection Miss Jones swayed eerily on the witness stand as though she might faint again on the spot, so that the clerk had to rush to her aid. Then Judge Freeman said in his kindly way that he thought there had been enough questions of Miss Jones for the time being. "However," he said to Mapleson, "of course, Counselor, you may cross-examine the witness later in the proceedings."

Dorset looked uneasy. He did not doubt that she was telling the truth, but her hysterical behavior did not make her the most reliable witness. It would be only natural for the defending attorney to question such a witness so as to make that clear to a judge or jury. He was therefore surprised when Mapleson replied, "Thank you, Your Honor, but I have no questions to ask Miss Jones."

Judge Freeman was also surprised. "You have no questions, Mr. Mapleson? You accept her testimony as it stands?"

"I see no reason to doubt that the witness reported what she saw in a substantially accurate way."

A questioning look appeared in the Judge's eyes. "Then, Mr. Dorset, you may proceed with your next witness."

The next witness was the impecabbly dressed, slightly rotund elderly gentleman seated at the back of the room. Prosecuting attorney Dorset began in the friendly voice he reserved for helpful witnesses: "Your name is Andrew Poole. Is that correct?"

"That is my name, sir," Poole replied in a correct, precise tone of voice; only a slight tremor betrayed the tension the man was feeling.

"Mr. Poole, please tell us your occupation."

"I have been a butler, sir."

"And for whom did you work?"

"My master was Dr. Henry Jekyll."

"Thank you. Then, of course, we can assume that you knew Dr. Jekyll quite well. Did you also know Mr. Edward Hyde?"

The butler paled visibly. "I did indeed, sir."

"Would you please tell the Court your impression of this man."

"I loathed him. I couldn't stand him. He spent much time with my master, locked away with him in my master's laboratory. I could not understand what my master ever saw in him."

"What was it about him that inspired your loathing?"

"It is hard to say. Perhaps his physical appearance—no, something about his manner, the expression on his face. I can only say that I never met a decent person who didn't hate Edward Hyde at first sight. And, I confess, I hated him too."

"Why did you hate him?"

"Because of the way he treated Dr. Jekyll, sir."

"And how was that?"

"He had some kind of power over him. He often visited the house and, as I have said, went into my master's laboratory to be alone with him. Hyde had great energy. He was an ugly man, sort of deformed, really, but he was younger than my master and had a certain youthful sprightliness about him. I felt that because of his greater energy he quite dominated my master. My master seemed rather hypnotized by him, as its victim is by a snake. After Hyde had left and I saw my master again he seemed diminished, weakened, and despite all his efforts to put on a good face I knew he was troubled and, yes, deeply frightened about something. It was Hyde who did this to him. When Hyde was around, my master got weaker, while Hyde seemed only to get stronger."

"I see. Is there anything more about Hyde that you can tell us?"

"Yes." Poole's voice was raised in obvious agitation. "It was Hyde who killed my good master! He killed him outright."

"Please tell the Court why you believe this to be so."

"Well, sir, my master had been acting strangely for many

months. It got worse and worse, quite intolerable. He would lock himself up in his laboratory and speak to us only through the door. We rarely saw him anymore. Yet sometimes I could hear through the closed door someone weeping and crying like a woman or a lost soul. When my master did come out, he was pale and drawn. As time went by, he shut himself away more and more. Once when he had been away for many days I went to the door and called in. A voice answered, but it was Hyde's voice, not my master's. More and more after that I heard the weeping voice inside the laboratory. I could not rid myself of the thought that there were foul deeds afoot and that something dreadful was happening to my master—indeed, that maybe he was now dead, since we saw him no more. I became so desperate that at last I went to see Mr. Utterson—"

"Do you see Mr. Utterson in the courtroom? If so, please point him out."

"Yes, Mr. Utterson is there, seated in the front row." And Poole pointed to the honest-looking man in the frock coat.

"Why did you think Mr. Utterson could help you?"

"Well, sir, Mr. Utterson is a lawyer, like yourself, and a more honest and capable gentleman you could not find anywhere. But more than that he was a devoted, longtime friend of my master's. I knew that Mr. Utterson would have the best interests of my master at heart and that I could trust him completely."

"I see. So what happened after you went to Mr. Utterson?"

"Well, at my urgent request Mr. Utterson went with me to the house. When we arrived the rest of the servants were overjoyed to see him. He came in like a savior, sir, like a veritable savior. One of the maids even wept and whimpered so that I had to command her to stop, for our nerves were already jangled enough without her wailing. Then I led Mr. Utterson through the back garden to my master's laboratory, and there together we knocked on the door. A muffled voice answered. I called out that Mr. Utterson wanted to see Dr. Jekyll. The voice answered, 'Tell him I cannot see anyone.' "

"Did that surprise you?"

"Not in itself, for my master had shut himself away from everyone like that for months. What surprised me—nay, shocked me deeply—was that it wasn't my master's voice. It was the voice of Edward Hyde."

"Are you certain?"

"I would have known Hyde's voice anywhere, sir. Besides, I had seen Hyde vanish into the laboratory only a few days before. I had come suddenly out into the garden and surprised someone rummaging around in the crates that stood there as though he was looking for something. I thought perhaps it was my master looking for some of the drug that he often sent me out to get. At his insistence I had gone to many chemist shops asking for a certain drug, but it never seemed to be the right one that I got, and the cartons of drugs I brought to him had been discarded in the garden. But when the man heard me and looked up I saw at once that he wasn't my master. True, he was dressed in my master's clothes; but this man was small and dwarfish, and the clothes hung on him like oversized bags. He wore a mask, so I couldn't see his face; but after he knew he'd been seen he kind of snarled and darted back into the laboratory, and I knew that it was Hyde."

"I see. Tell the Court what you and Utterson did after you thought you heard Hyde, instead of Dr. Jekyll, answer your call through the door."

"We both feared the worst, so we decided to break down the door."

"And did you?"

"We did. We took an ax and split the door apart and pushed through and burst into . . . "

"What did you see?"

"There, in the midst of the debris that once was my master's fine laboratory, twitching on the floor, contorted in death, was Edward Hyde—all dressed in my master's clothes—and there was no sign of my master."

Dorset paused to let this dismaying testimony sink in. "Mr.

Poole, I know it has been hard on you to recall this dreadful scene, but I must ask you one or two more questions. As you know, it is common belief that your master and Edward Hyde were, somehow, one and the same person, or, you might better say, two persons living in one body and one soul. Do you believe that?"

"I do not, sir!"

"Why not?"

"Why, my master was a good man, of genial disposition, always trying to please others, a man who regarded his reputation as of the utmost importance. If anything, he went rather too far in courting the goodwill and favor of others. But this Hyde was loathesome and utterly selfish and ruthless, nor did he care the slightest what others thought of him. He seemed to relish being hated, and I am sure he scorned my master's predilection for the admiration of others. I cannot believe they were one and the same person. But it doesn't matter, you know. If Hyde was one man and my master another, then Hyde murdered my master and mysteriously did away with the body. And if it's true that Hyde was somehow also my master, he murdered him just the same, because he killed my master's better nature, destroyed it bit by bit and ground it into the dust until he had taken him over body and soul. So either way you have it, I say that Edward Hyde murdered Henry Jekyll."

"Thank you, Poole," Dorset said. Then, glancing at Mapleson with the glint of triumph in his eyes, he said with a note of disdain, "Your witness, Counselor."

Poole waited nervously as Dorset took his seat alongside his two colleagues at the table. Judge Freeman turned his eyes on Mapleson. Dr. Savant, Dr. Christiansen, Mr. Weatherford, and Ms. Wood stirred uneasily in their chairs as they waited for Mapleson's cross-examination of this witness who had produced such damaging testimony. Mapleson stood: "I have no questions of the witness, Your Honor."

There was a shocked silence. The faces of those in the jury box looked puzzled. Triumph flashed in Dorset's eyes and he seemed to be thinking, "He knows he's licked; he can think of nothing to do." Judge Freeman, however, was angry.

"Mr. Mapleson," he declared, "I must remind you not to toy with this Court. You have heard three witnesses produce the most damaging possible testimony against your client. All have accused him of the most heinous crimes, indeed, have virtually identified him with evil incarnate. You have asked us for this hearing to defend Hyde against exactly these charges, yet you refuse to ask questions of any of the witnesses. I warn you, if it should prove that you are taking this matter lightly, engaging, perhaps, in some mysterious game of your own, I will do my utmost to see to it that you never again are allowed to be heard before this Court."

"Your Honor," Mapleson replied humbly, "I can understand your irritation. I assure you that I do not take this Court lightly. I will in time call on the persons who have taken the witness stand and ask them questions, but I will summon them as my witnesses. This is why I do not cross-examine them now as witnesses of Mr. Dorset."

"This means, then, that you are accepting their stories as they stand? That you do not challenge the veracity or accuracy of their recollections?"

"It means that I accept their stories as they stand."

Judge Freeman's face registered disbelief. "Call the next witness," he ordered brusquely.

Mr. Utterson took the stand. Lawyer and scholar, he had none of the nervousness of Enfield, the hysterical anguish of the maid, or the pitiable distress of Poole. His face radiated honest and deep concern for the truth. Clearly his testimony would carry great weight.

Dorset began. "Mr. Utterson, you are, I believe, a friend of Mr. Richard Enfield?"

"Yes, that is the case. A friend of longstanding."

"You have heard his testimony. Do you believe it to be true?"

"I was not, of course, present when my friend Enfield saw Hyde trample the young girl, but I have no doubt that this happened substantially as Mr. Enfield reported it."

"Did you yourself ever see Mr. Hyde?"

"Indeed. Of course Enfield told me his story. What he had to say was of uncommon interest to me because, as you must know, I was Henry Jekyll's attorney and I was aware that Edward Hyde was named as beneficiary in my client's will. I had always wondered who this strange Mr. Hyde was, and now I had reason to be suspicious of him. So I made it a point to see Hyde for myself. For this purpose I waited many days near the door to Henry Jekyll's house until Hyde finally appeared. I had no difficulty in recognizing him; he fit exactly the description given by Mr. Enfield."

"What was your impression of Hyde?"

"My impression confirmed everything Enfield had told me. Hyde was a man to inspire the utmost loathing upon the mere sight of him. I've never seen a more hateful face, and, as has been said, his body gave the impression of deformity, though it was hard to say exactly why. Yet there was nothing sickly about him. To the contrary, he walked lightly and seemed to possess an uncommon amount of physical energy."

"Mr. Utterson, you have also heard the testimony of Miss Jones. Can you verify her testimony?"

"Well, of course I was not present at the time of the murder, but it so happened that I knew the victim. The kindly old man whom the maid, Miss Jones, saw so brutally murdered was my friend and client, Dr. Danvers Carew. Indeed, a legal document bearing my name was found by the police on his corpse, and as a consequence I was called in on the case. I saw Dr. Carew's beaten and crumpled body and have no reason to doubt that the testimony of Miss Jones about how it happened is accurate. The police asked me to accompany them in their investigation, and we went to the house where Hyde was said to reside in Soho. He had fled, which certainly points to his guilt, and we were greeted only by his evil-faced landlady, who would only tell us that he had gone."

Dorset spoke, "Mr. Utterson, Mr. Poole has testified that he came to you and asked for your help, and that you accompanied him to the house and then went to the door of Henry Jekyll's

laboratory. He said that when you called and it was Hyde who
answered, you broke into the laboratory to find Hyde's body
twitching in death from what appeared to be suicide. Is this in
fact what happened?"

"It is all true."

"Can you add anything to the testimony of these persons?"

"Yes. After the death of my friend Henry Jekyll I read two
letters. One had been given to me some time before by our mutual friend Dr. Lanyon. The second was in the laboratory, addressed to me, written by Henry Jekyll shortly before his
demise."

"Have the contents of these letters a bearing on our case?"

"They do indeed. They substantiate, I would say, the charges
against Edward Hyde. They make it clear that Hyde was responsible not only for the death of Jekyll but also for the unfortunate death of Lanyon."

"Please tell us what the letters revealed."

"Well, Dr. Jekyll, as you must know, had a great scientific interest in perfecting a drug that would enable him to assume for
the time being a personality somewhat different from his own.
This other personality that he wished to use was, so he
thought, harmless enough, but enjoyed certain pursuits in life
that were not in keeping with the reputation my friend had so
carefully cultivated for himself. It seems that Jekyll did indeed
succeed in devising such a drug. When he took the drug he was
changed into this other self; when he took it again he resumed
his former personality. Tragically, however, this other personality turned out to be more evil than Jekyll had imagined. He
was, of course, none other than Edward Hyde, and he came, as
time went on, to take over Jekyll more and more. At first Hyde
only appeared when Jekyll had ingested the drug, but eventually Hyde acquired the ability to take over Jekyll at any time—
even in the most embarrassing situations, such as in a public
park—and all without the good doctor's so willing it. This became a great problem after the murder of Dr. Carew, for henceforth Jekyll dared not be seen in public in the guise of Edward

Hyde. Indeed, when he was in the form of Hyde he dared not even approach his laboratory where the drug was kept that he relied upon to restore him to himself. So it happened that in his extremity he had to ask for help from our mutual friend Dr. Lanyon. He sent Lanyon a note, beseeching him to go to the laboratory and return to meet him at midnight with the desired potion. Lanyon, of course, knew nothing of the purposes for which Jekyll desired the drug, and out of loyalty to his friend, obtained it and returned home. At the hour of midnight Hyde appeared and demanded the drug. Then, so Lanyon wrote, Hyde, with a dreadful leering look, said Lanyon might care to watch what happened next. With that, Hyde took the drug and right in front of Lanyon's eyes was transformed into Jekyll. The whole thing was too much for Lanyon. He never recovered from the shock, and within a few weeks he was dead. Hyde could just as well have taken the drug in private; it was out of pure malice that he bade Lanyon look at what was going to happen. Therefore I hold Hyde responsible for Lanyon's death."

A hushed silence in the courtroom greeted this chilling testimony. Even the tough-minded Ralph Dorset seemed taken aback. At length he resumed his questioning: "And the letter left by Henry Jekyll?"

"The contents of this letter, of course, have now been published, and anyone can examine it. Therein Henry Jekyll revealed all. He told how he had, as I have already said, long desired to live from time to time out of what he called a certain impatient gaiety of disposition, but that he feared to do so lest his reputation be damaged. He reported that it was for this reason he devised the transformative drug, for when he was in the guise of Edward Hyde he could do what he liked and no one would hold Henry Jekyll responsible. He had no idea that Hyde was as evil as he was, and when he realized that, he tried his utmost to rid himself of Hyde, although he confesses he always had a secret longing for Hyde in spite of everything. Hyde, however, never had any desire to live as Jekyll. To the

contrary, so we learn from the letter, Hyde plotted Jekyll's destruction and was wont to curse both Jekyll and even God himself with the worst blasphemies. In his effort to rid himself of
Hyde, my friend Henry Jekyll turned to religion, and performed good deeds so as to win the gratitude of many and
please the Almighty. But none of this seemed to help. Hyde
gained in strength in spite of Jekyll's prayers and good deeds
and seemed to consume Jekyll's will and spirit. Thus Hyde
waxed stronger as Jekyll became weaker. The end of Jekyll's
letter was most pitiable. He wrote that this letter was the last
act that he, Henry Jekyll, would perform on this earth. He fully
anticipated that very soon Hyde would take him over once
more and he would never again resume his former appearance.
So it turned out to be, and for this reason, when we broke into
the laboratory, we saw twitching in death on the floor the body
of Edward Hyde. Jekyll had been destroyed. In effect, Hyde, in
his malice, murdered him."

A solemn hush lay heavy in the room. Dorset broke the silence. "Thank you, Mr. Utterson, thank you for that clear testimony." Then, turning with a look of obvious triumph at Mapleson, he said, "Your witness, Mr. Mapleson."

Surely the defending attorney would cross-examine this witness! But Mapleson rose to his full, lanky height and simply
said, "I have no questions, Your Honor."

Dorset sprang to his feet. "Your Honor! My worthy opponent's conduct in this case is deplorable. We have all heard the
most damaging possible testimony against Edward Hyde. It is
obvious that Hyde, a hateful and evil man, was responsible for
the brutal treatment of an innocent child, for the malicious
murder of a respected elderly gentleman, and for the destruction of two eminent people, Dr. Lanyon and Dr. Jekyll. It is also
clear that this Hyde had not the slightest twinge of conscience
in the matter, and that, at least in the case of Jekyll, his murders
were premeditated. In view of the fact that Mapleson appears
to have no defense to offer, I request that Your Honor consider
rendering your judgment now and saving the many fine peo-

ple who have come here in good faith the loss of any more of their time—"

Now Mapleson was on his feet. "Your Honor, I object. My worthy opponent has said that I have no defense to offer, but that is not so. That I do not challenge the witnesses who have appeared to testify against Hyde does not mean I have no defense to make. If it please the Court, if the prosecuting attorney has called his last witness, I will call witnesses of my own and proceed to make my case."

The courtroom was in an uproar. Dorset's charges against Mapleson had sent through the room a ripple of anger against the defending attorney, and murmurs of "yes" and "let it be so" could be heard when Dorset called for a speedy judgment. Mapleson's remarks were greeted with marked skepticism. Judge Freeman had to rap for silence. At length he spoke to Mapleson, "Mr. Mapleson, you will be allowed to call your witnesses. But let me warn you that if you toy with this Court and with the justice that it seeks to dispense I will hold you in contempt. However, we have all heard quite enough for today. I declare the Court in recess until tomorrow morning at nine."

Judge Freeman gathered together his papers. The clerk opened the door to his private chambers, and soon the imposing figure of the Judge disappeared. Slowly, still in a state of some shock at recent testimony and events, the gallery emptied. Dr. Savant joined with the crowd and exited. Dr. Christiansen and Mr. Weatherford also departed. Dorset and his aides shot a disdainful look at Mapleson and went out, talking animatedly together. Only Ms. Wood and Mr. Mapleson remained. Ms. Wood looked at Mapleson as though she wanted to say something but could not quite bring herself to do so. At last she too departed, her trim, graceful figure disappearing through the great doors at the back. Mapleson's eyes followed her as she left. He sat alone for some time, his head in his hands. Then he slowly gathered his papers and put them in his briefcase, and he too left the room.

# 3 Mapleson Takes a Turn and Dorset Concludes His Argument

The morning sun found its way through the city's grime on the windows and made bright patches on the floor of the courtroom. Court was again in session. All were in their places: the Judge at the bench, Dorset and his aides at their table, the four advisers, Savant, Christiansen, Weatherford, and Ms. Wood, in the jury box. The gallery was close to being filled; perhaps word had gone round that something a bit out of the ordinary was going on.

"Your Honor, I wish to call Mr. Andrew Poole as my first witness." It was Mapleson speaking, opening his case at last.

Andrew Poole, impeccably dressed as usual, took the witness stand and was duly sworn in by the clerk. "Mr. Poole," Mapleson began gently, "do you by any chance have in your possession one of your master's calling cards?"

Judge Freeman interrupted, "I find that an odd question, Counselor. I must remind you again not to dally with the Court." It was clear that the good Judge was still irritated with Mapleson's performance of the day before.

"Quite right, Your Honor. I can assure you that I have good reason for wanting to see one of Henry Jekyll's calling cards."

"Very well, Counselor. Please answer the question, Mr. Poole."

Poole spoke. "Well, sir, now why should I have one of Dr. Jekyll's calling cards now that he is gone? Yet, well, perhaps I do. I used to carry extras in my wallet, just in case they were ever needed . . . Yes, I believe I do . . . here . . ." and Poole offered Mapleson a worn, folded card.

"That's all right, Mr. Poole. You keep the card. But please read to the Court how Henry Jekyll has written his name."

"Why, 'Henry Jekyll,' of course."

"What has he put after his name?"

"Well, he had various degrees, you know, both earned and honorary."

"Would you please read them to us—just the way they appear on the card."

" 'Henry Jekyll, M.D., D.C.L, LL.D, F.R.S., and several others I can't make out just now because the card is old and faded."

"That seems like quite a few degrees, does it not? What do these initials stand for?"

"Well, M.D., of course, was because he was a medical doctor, and very proud of it too, I might add. 'LL.D' was, I believe, for his work in literature; he was an extremely literate man—often spoke at literary gatherings. The others, well, upon my word, I don't know what they all stand for, honorary degrees, I believe . . . he set great store by them."

"Would you say, then, that Henry Jekyll was a man who was unusually concerned about his reputation?"

"Quite, sir. He enjoyed a good reputation and worked hard to be well thought of, but if you are suggesting that he did not deserve the high regard in which he was held, you are quite mistaken."

"I am sure he worked hard for his reputation, Mr. Poole. Tell me, on what do you think this reputation was based?"

"Well, sir, my master was a man of means, you know, which won him the respect of the poor and the admiration of the wealthy. He was uncommonly industrious in his social pursuits, being fond of the respect of the wise and good among his fellows, and had a most distinguished past and future ahead of him."

"Thank you, Mr. Poole. Only one more question, was Henry Jekyll married?"

"No."

"Had he ever been married?"

"Never, to the best of my knowledge."

Poole left the witness stand and resumed his chair. The advisers in the jury box had listened passively, as though their minds were already made up, except for Melanie Wood, whose face registered a quizzical expression.

Mr. Richard Enfield was Mapleson's next witness. Mercifully for the nervous Mr. Enfield, his stay on the witness stand was brief. "Mr. Enfield," Mapleson began, "you have told us how you met Edward Hyde. Did you also know Henry Jekyll?"

"Not well. I only met him briefly a few times."

"Did you know him by reputation?"

"Oh, indeed."

"Could you describe his reputation for us?"

"Well, he was quite celebrated among the upper echelons of medical and literary society, with a few exceptions, of course. And social, too. He cultivated his friendships carefully. He went about doing a great deal of what I suppose you would call good, and this won him the admiration of many people."

"You say there were exceptions. Of whom are you thinking?"

"Well, Dr. Lanyon, for instance, questioned the wisdom of Jekyll's experiments, and I suppose considering how things turned out he was right, though Dr. Jekyll, of course, maintained that it was all in the interest of science."

"Thank you, Mr. Enfield. Two final questions. Are you married?"

Enfield seemed slightly irritated. "I have never been married, sir."

"And Dr. Lanyon, was he married?"

"Never, to the best of my knowledge."

As Enfield resumed his seat in the gallery, Dorset rose and addressed the Judge. "Your Honor, I object to these proceedings. We are here to determine the guilt or innocence of Edward Hyde. I regard these inquiries into the private reputation of Henry Jekyll intrusive and irrelevant, and the marital status of Jekyll and others associated with him is of no concern to this Court."

"Your objection is understandable, Mr. Dorset. Counselor, will you please make your questions more germane in future."

Mapleson rejoined, "Your Honor, I can understand your position, but I beg the patience of the Court as I question the next witness, Mr. Utterson, for I sincerely believe that the questions I am asking are important for the defense of Edward Hyde."

Utterson, himself an attorney, might have been a difficult witness, but he was a man who first and foremost valued the truth and he answered Mapleson's questions solemnly and with candor, even though the first question must have annoyed him.

"Mr. Utterson, are you married?"

"I am not."

"Mr. Poole told us that Dr. Lanyon was not married either. How about Dr. Carew? or even Edward Hyde? Do you know if any of the persons mentioned by any of the witnesses were married or had close relationships with the other sex?"

Ms. Wood leaned forward in her chair so as not to miss any of Utterson's reply.

"None was married. Hyde lived in a rooming house in Soho run by a fearsome-looking woman who greeted myself and the police, as I have mentioned, in a most unfriendly way when we inquired after him. It would be too much to suggest that they had anything like a close relationship."

"Mr. Utterson, will you please tell the Court how long you knew Henry Jekyll, and the nature of his reputation."

"I knew Jekyll for many years. As a young man he was what you might call a bit on the wild side. Nothing serious, but he liked the sensual pleasures of this life perhaps just a bit too much. As he matured this tendency vanished, and he lived a life of great respectability."

"His extensive use of degrees after his name would seem to indicate that Henry Jekyll was a man who was eager to create a certain impression. Would you agree with that?"

"I think that is accurate. He wanted others to see him in a favorable light. To this end he cultivated an air of what you might call genial respectability. The degrees after his name enhanced all that, I'm sure. He was well known, you see, and highly considered, and that was certainly important to him. However, you must realize that he worked hard to merit and deserve this reputation."

"I am not disputing that, of course. Now, Mr. Utterson, you have testified that before Jekyll died he wrote a final letter in which he gave the full particulars of this unusual case. This letter was entrusted to you, and you were the one to read it in its original form. Would you please tell the Court how Henry Jekyll saw Edward Hyde?"

"As evil. He believed Hyde was evil. Indeed, he was shocked to find Hyde ten times more evil than he ever thought he would be. He saw Hyde's every action centered on himself and himself alone. There is no question but that Jekyll disliked and feared Hyde greatly."

"How did Jekyll view himself?"

"Of course, he did not see himself as perfect. He was aware of certain failings in himself. Perhaps the most important was his awareness that, in spite of his intense dislike of Hyde and fear of him, he also felt a certain attraction to him. But in spite of all that, I think Jekyll concurred in the opinion of his friends and acquaintances that he was a good and genial man."

"You mentioned Jekyll's attraction to Hyde. What do you think was the basis of it?"

"Extremely hard to see, but perhaps it was Hyde's youthfulness. Hyde, for all his dwarfish size and malformed appearance, was remarkably energetic, whereas my friend Henry Jekyll, like many of us who reach the age of fifty, was losing some of his vitality, exhausted, no doubt, by his life of virtuous and dedicated service."

"If Henry Jekyll perceived Hyde to be so evil, then why do you think he had anything to do with him, even granting that Jekyll was getting older and longed for a touch of Hyde's youth?"

"Well, of course, Henry Jekyll believed himself to be innocent. No matter what Hyde did, he believed that Hyde and Hyde alone was guilty. Jekyll did not believe that Hyde's misdeeds diminished Jekyll's own good qualities, in which he believed and trusted to the very end."

"To the very end?"

"Indeed. In the last lines of the letter to which you have referred Jekyll referred to Hyde as 'another than myself.' I take this to be evidence of my friend's fundamental good intentions and devout nature."

"You say that Henry Jekyll believed himself to be good even at the end. Yet is it not true, that after the murder of Dr. Carew, Jekyll referred to himself as 'the chief of sinners' and also 'the chief of sufferers'?"

"He had occasional lapses into remorse, of course, but they did not last. No, he saw sinfulness in Hyde, but not for long in himself, for, quite understandably, he believed in his own good intentions. As for his suffering, of this he was convinced, though I suppose when he called himself the 'chief of sufferers' that must be taken as an exaggeration, for who can say how much everyone else has suffered?"

Mapleson continued. "Now, as time went on, as you have testified previously, Jekyll came to fear Hyde more and more because Hyde had the power to take possession of him whenever he chose to do so. Could you elaborate on the reason for Jekyll's fear?"

"Well, of course, Jekyll repudiated Hyde's evil for the most part, and so Hyde horrified him. But there was also the matter of Jekyll's reputation. Especially after the murder of Dr. Carew, he feared his secret alliance with Hyde would be exposed, and then, of course, his hard-won reputation would be shattered. That all seems natural enough."

"Natural, of course. Now, Mr. Utterson, you will remember that, after the murder of Dr. Carew, Henry Jekyll determined to have nothing more to do with Hyde. Is that correct?"

"Quite correct. He had had enough of Hyde. He told me that

he could do away with him anytime he wished, and after he saw how evil and destructive Hyde was he determined to do so. From that time on my friend devoted himself to good works more assiduously than ever before. He tried his best to undo the evil that had been done. He even became religious into the bargain, which was new to him, for though he had always done more than his share of good in the world, he had not been noted for what might be called a religious nature. Now this too changed, and people were startled and pleased to hear Henry Jekyll talking a great deal about God."

"Yet in spite of all this Jekyll could not keep Hyde from appearing again and again?"

"Unfortunately, that is so."

"Do you remember Jekyll's description of the first time that it became evident to Jekyll that Hyde could take him over even against his will?"

"Indeed. Jekyll gave full particulars in his letter. He was sitting innocently on a park bench when the change took place and, to his horror, in spite of all his resistance, he became Hyde."

"But was there not something else in Jekyll's account? Something going on in his mind at the time?"

"Let me see . . . Yes, I do recall. Jekyll wrote that just before Hyde reappeared he had been comparing what he called his active goodwill, for this was during a time of his greatest activity in doing good, with what he termed the 'lazy cruelty and neglect of the greater part of mankind.' It was right after that that he experienced nausea and began shuddering and Hyde possessed him again."

In the jury box, Mr. Weatherford looked agitated. He straightened his tie and cleared his throat, and for a moment it looked as though he might say something, but perhaps fearing that he would be out of place, he kept silent as Mapleson continued his questions

"Mr. Utterson, you have told us how Jekyll viewed Hyde. Can you tell us now how Hyde saw your friend Dr. Jekyll?"

"There can be no doubt that Hyde despised him. Henry Jekyll, with good reason, believed that Hyde rejected him entirely and devoted great efforts to punishing him. He believed that Hyde would gladly have ruined himself in order to ruin him, that in Hyde he had an implacable enemy."

"It has been asserted that Hyde's actions were wantonly, senselessly evil. Would you go so far as to say that Hyde did, then, have at least one purpose: the destruction of Henry Jekyll?"

Dorset was on his feet. "I object, Your Honor! Counselor is leading the witness."

"Objections sustained," said Judge Freeman. "Counselor, you must rephrase your question."

"Certainly. Mr. Utterson, do you believe that Hyde's actions had a purpose in them as far as Jekyll was concerned?"

"I would have to say that was so. That was certainly Henry Jekyll's belief." Utterson seemed lost in reflection for a few moments. "That may be why Henry saw the murder of Carew not only as a brutal but as a tragic folly, because this, more than anything else Hyde did, brought destruction of destroying Jekyll?"

"Are you suggesting then, Mr. Utterson, that when Hyde murdered Carew he did it with the intention of destroying Jekyll?"

"I cannot go that far. We do not know what was in Hyde's mind except as we can infer it from his actions, and from Jekyll's own suppositions. Let us just say that Jekyll believed Hyde was out to destroy him, and this action of Hyde's, more than perhaps any other, achieved that general purpose."

"But how could Hyde destroy Jekyll when Jekyll was a man of stature and distinction, highly respected, educated, industrious, all in all an important person to the whole community, whereas Hyde was a dwarfish, unknown man?"

"Well, Hyde, you see, so Henry himself wrote, was getting stronger all the time, while Jekyll was getting weaker."

"Mr. Utterson, a little while ago you said that, after the murder of Dr. Carew, Henry Jekyll went about doing more good than ever, and also became religious. Could you tell us more about your friend's religion?"

It was now Dr. Christiansen's turn to look uneasy in the jury box. He bent forward in his chair as though he did not wish to miss any of Utterson's answer.

"As I have indicated, earlier in his life Jekyll did not talk much about God, and if he had a sense of the divine Presence he said nothing about it. But after he felt Hyde's power he became sincerely religious. He attended church often, though he never joined, and he often spoke of God and regarded his good deeds as done to please the Almighty."

"This was apparent to others?"

"Oh, indeed. It became generally known that Henry Jekyll, always distinguished for his charitable actions, was now no less distinguished for his devotion to religion."

"Thank you, Mr. Utterson. Your Honor, I have no more witnesses to call."

There was a stir in the courtroom. The Judge rapped for attention. "Mr. Dorset," he asked, "do you have any questions to ask the witness?"

"None, Your Honor," Dorset replied.

"Then are you ready to present your closing argument?"

"I am."

"Please proceed." Was the Judge tiring of Mapleson's seemingly irrelevant questions? He seemed impatient to reach a conclusion.

With his powerful body, Dorset moved in like a panther ready for the kill, positioning himself so he could speak to the Judge but also to the panel of experts.

"Your Honor, we heard four witnesses yesterday morning testify to the infamous crimes committed by Edward Hyde. Mr. Enfield told us of Hyde's brutal assault on an innocent young girl. Miss Jones testified that she witnessed Hyde's unprovoked murder of the elderly Dr. Danvers Carew. Mr. Poole and Mr. Utterson both informed us that Hyde terrorized the household of Dr. Jekyll, caused the death of the esteemed Dr. Lanyon by his callous disregard for human sensibilities, and deliberately destroyed his finer counterpart, Henry Jekyll.

"We have all heard the testimony, yet no voice has been raised to challenge it. The counselor for the defense has not even seen fit to cross-examine the witnesses. It must therefore be assumed that the criminal allegations against Edward Hyde go uncontested.

"Your Honor, and ladies and gentlemen in this courtroom," Dorset turned for a moment to face the advisers and the gallery, "no decent society can allow, condone, or forgive such crimes as this man Edward Hyde has committed. It is for this reason that the universal judgment of humanity has condemned him. Such condemnation is just and correct. Indeed," with a quick glance at Mapleson, "the moral integrity of anyone who fails to agree in this judgment is seriously open to question.

"Hyde is beyond the reach of the just punishment that society should inflict upon him for his crimes, but it is in the power of this Court to condemn Hyde without mercy, even as he showed no mercy to his victims. This should be done, not in the spirit of vindictiveness, but to discourage further evil on the part of others. For though it is true that it is not within human power to eradicate evil, it is also true that it is in our power to minimize evil and its effects by punishing it whenever it makes its appearance. If this Court should choose to exonerate Edward Hyde it could only serve to encourage the evil impulses in generations to come. For this reason I urge Hyde's speedy and complete condemnation."

Dorset resumed his seat. His aides whispered approvingly into his ear. A satisfied smile crossed his face, a smile like that of a chess player who is certain he has checkmated his opponent. A low ripple of talk went through the gallery, and here and there someone grunted approval or said "amen." But Mapleson's final argument had not yet been heard, nor had the advisers spoken their minds.

Judge Freeman spoke. "Mr. Mapleson, the fair hearing you asked for your client has been granted. You have heard the arguments against him. This Court has given generously of its time. You have chosen not to challenge any of the testimony against Edward Hyde. If you have anything to say in his defense, now is the time for you to speak."

Mapleson answered. "Your Honor, I do indeed have much to say. But we have all heard great and weighty testimony. Also, we have not yet heard from the members of our council of experts, who may have things they wish to say. I would like to request a recess of this Court until tomorrow, to allow me time to gather my final thoughts and take into consideration all that we have heard so far."

The Judge did not look pleased, but, fair-minded man that he was, he considered the request. "Mr. Mapleson, I feel you have had ample time to plan your argument; for this reason I will not postpone our proceedings until tomorrow. However, out of deference to the needs you express, I declare this Court in recess until this afternoon at one o'clock."

# 4 Unexpected Interruptions

The clock chimed one. Enfield, Utterson, Poole, Miss Jones—all were in their accustomed seats. The advisers sat stiffly. The Reverend Dr. Christiansen had arrived first, punctiliously prompt; Mr. Weatherford still looked ill at ease; Dr. Savant was studiously relaxed; Melanie Wood's face was a study in keen anticipation. Dorset and his aides sat together at their table. Mapleson sat alone. The gallery was now almost full. No sooner had the final echoes of the clock's bell ended than the door from the Judge's private chambers opened and the clerk entered, with Judge Freeman a few steps behind. All rose. The Judge rapped for attention and declared that the Court was now in session. When all were seated he spoke.

"Mr. Mapleson, I trust that we will now hear your concluding argument, for the fair hearing that you asked for your client has been granted. You have heard the accusations against him, and this Court has given generously of its time. If you have anything to say in his defense this is the time for you to speak."

Mapleson rose. All eyes were on him. Some glared at him; some were merely curious. He spoke. "Your Honor, and ladies and gentlemen of this Court, I do not deny the facts that have been presented documenting the misdeeds of Edward Hyde, nor do I deny that they are heinous crimes. It is not the deeds that I am questioning, but the cause of the deeds, for only when this has been established can we determine the proper guilt and punishment to be apportioned to the principals in this case. It is my contention that, though Edward Hyde was the instrumental cause of the crimes so ably summarized for us by Mr. Dorset, he was not the original or ultimate cause. I propose to argue that the origin of the evil that Hyde was forced to act out lay elsewhere. I will make two points: first, that there was another person whose evil was greater than that of Hyde, second, that Hyde was the instrument of a power greater than himself. I will not claim that Hyde was entirely without blame. But I will argue that greater blame lay elsewhere, and that the judgment upon Hyde, though it is not to be entirely withdrawn, must therefore be mitigated. Let us ask ourselves: If several people owe one million dollars, is it fair that society demand the entire debt be paid by only one of them? Certainly not. We would all agree, in the interest of justice, that if many persons owe a debt they all be required to pay. It will be my contention that the case we are considering is analogous."

The Judge interrupted. "I heard you say, Mr. Mapleson, that you believe others to be as responsible for the evil as Hyde. In fact, I heard you say that others, or at least someone else, was more responsible than Hyde insofar as that person originated the evil. I believe I also heard you say that Hyde, though he did evil, was the instrument of some mysterious power. These are serious allegations you are making: I trust you have an equally serious argument to support them."

Mapleson replied, "Thank you, Your Honor. You have heard me correctly. With your permission I will now proceed to support my argument. We have heard the testimony against Edward Hyde. However, we have also heard unwitting testimony about Henry Jekyll. I would call your attention to the kind of man exemplified in Henry Jekyll—to the essence, if you like, of his character. Let us begin with the matter of his calling card, seemingly a slight matter but in fact quite revealing. His calling card, with its impressive array of degrees after his name, attests not so much to his accomplishments as to the inflated idea of himself that Henry Jekyll entertained and to the way he wished others to regard him. One would suppose that the simple, but earned degree of doctor of medicine would have sufficed—but no! Henry Jekyll had to add after it degrees so numerous and obscure that not even his servant of long standing, Mr. Poole, could tell us what they meant.

"Consider also that Henry Jekyll was not and never had been married; nor was there any woman who was a part of his personal life. For that matter, neither was there a woman in the life of Mr. Utterson or Dr. Lanyon. We are forced to conclude that Henry Jekyll failed in that fundamental task that falls on almost every man to relate to, love, and give himself in camaraderie to a person of the opposite sex, and that the friends he chose also would appear to have failed in this regard.

"Consider further Dr. Jekyll's reputation as we have learned about it from Mr. Enfield. Jekyll cultivated for himself the reputation of being a good and upstanding man. Enfield, to use his exact words, said that he was a man who went about doing what we usually call good. This, I submit, is not testimony about a good man but about a man who *appeared* to be good, who was in fact a sham, hollow like the inside of a tree that appears from the outside to be sound but is rotten and diseased on the inside.

"There is also the testimony of Mr. Utterson in this regard. Mr. Utterson was Jekyll's closest and most loyal friend; he is a man of honesty and integrity on whom we can rely for a fair and objective appraisal. Now, Mr. Utterson tells us of Jekyll's eminence among his fellows, yet he also tells us that Jekyll cultivated a certain posture that he referred to as an 'air of genial respectability.'

"These matters might seem at first glance to be relatively minor flaws in Jekyll's character, save for their effect on Edward Hyde. Consider now the attitude of Henry Jekyll toward Edward Hyde, and of Hyde's attitude toward him. Jekyll saw Hyde as evil. When he realized the capacity of Hyde for evil, and the acute embarrassment this might cause him, he wished to be rid of him. Yet by Jekyll's own testimony, as revealed to us in the letter left to Mr. Utterson, Jekyll told us that he experienced a certain longing for Hyde even as he feared him. There was therefore a strange connection between the two based upon their *common evil!*"

At Mapleson's stress on the words *common evil*, Weatherford visibly squirmed in his seat. Mapleson continued, "Now, by the testimony we have heard, we know that Jekyll's energy was diminishing, that he was in fact close to exhaustion. Was it Hyde's youth that attracted him? Was he willing to experience Hyde's youthful energy even if the price he paid was also to experience Hyde's evil? A callous thought! Yet, except for brief expressions of a conscience born more out of fear of punishment than conviction of what is right and wrong, Henry Jekyll believed firmly in his own innocence. He never accepted Hyde as a person for whom he too was responsible: indeed, at the very end of his life, in the aforesaid letter to Utterson, he referred to Hyde as 'another than myself.'

"Oh, to be sure, occasionally Jekyll had fits of what could be called remorse. These, however, did not spring from moral sensibility, but from a fear of exposure and punishment. And when he did castigate himself he used language as inflated and self-serving as the language he used in praise of himself. Vaingloriously he once referred to himself as 'the chief of sinners' and then, in self-pitying tones, as 'the chief of sufferers.' These extreme statements spring not from humility, but from the longing for grandeur that characterized him. If he could not be the greatest saint, then he would be the greatest sinner—yet not in his eyes a genuine sinner, but the innocent victim of a suffering imposed on him from without.

"As for Hyde's actions, Jekyll deplored them, but more because of their potential for damage to his reputation than because of concern for Hyde's victims. For example, consider the events that led up to that fateful moment when Hyde possessed Jekyll without benefit of the drug, thus demonstrating his increasing power over him. Jekyll sat in the park, you will recall, content in the illusion that he had done with Hyde forever. And what was he thinking? That he, Henry Jekyll, surpassed his fellow human beings in goodwill, and that his assiduous pursuit of good deeds was a clear sign of his superiority to the lazy neglect and cruelty of the greater part of humanity! Note that it was immediately after these self-serving thoughts that

Edward Hyde possessed Jekyll once again, and this time without benefit of the drug. This demonstrates that just such thoughts as these were the instrumental cause that gave Edward Hyde his power—"

"OUTRAGEOUS!" It was Weatherford, on his feet glaring at Mapleson, his voice resounding through the courtroom like the shock wave from a sonic boom. "Absolutely outrageous! Mapleson, we are here to try Edward Hyde, not Henry Jekyll, but you, ignoring Hyde and his obvious guilt, are droning on and on about the supposed failings of Henry Jekyll. You recite what appears to you to be a list of heinous crimes: he did what appeared to be good deeds, he liked degrees after his name, he did not marry, he was fond of a genial reputation. These minor misdemeanors of Henry Jekyll are nothing compared to the crimes of Edward Hyde! Why do you waste our time?

"As for Jekyll, thank God that there are people like him in this world who do care what others think of them, and who want to do good. Do you not realize, sir, that in accusing the good Dr. Jekyll you are accusing the greater part of humanity? Do not all respectable people value their reputation in the eyes of others? Those of us who seek virute in life devote our energies to God, even as Henry Jekyll did, and you have the infamy to imply that we are responsible for the crimes of the wicked. As for the fact that Henry Jekyll prided himself on his good deeds and then Edward Hyde took him over—is it not right and desirable that those of us who do good find satisfaction in so doing? I say Hyde possessed Jekyll at that time because the devil could not stand the good that lived in Henry Jekyll. If Jekyll's be a crime, then let us pray God that we have more of it—"

Judge Freeman rapped loudly with his gavel, but Weatherford kept on with his torrent of words until at last he began to sputter like an engine running out of gas. The Judge rapped sternly again, and at last Weatherford slumped back into his seat. "Mr. Weatherford," the Judge declared, "I can understand that you are upset by the line of argument the counselor is taking, but this Court must proceed by rules and your remarks are out of order. However errant Mr. Mapleson's line of argument may seem to you, he has not finished. Please maintain your silence. In time you will have your chance to speak. Now, Mr. Mapleson, please proceed. Be expeditious and make your points quickly."

Mapleson did not seem distrubed by Weatherford's outburst. "Your Honor, if it please the Court, I will be happy for Mr. Weatherford to finish what he has to say at this time. Provided I am allowed to eventually conclude my argument, it is agreeable to me if Weatherford, or any of the other experts on our panel, interrupt to make their points. In fact, this departure from custom could allow for a dialogue that would be a crucible from which the truth could emerge."

The Judge pondered this remarkable and generous offer. "Then you don't care if you are interrupted?"

"I do not care as long as eventually I can finish my point."

"I see. Well, it's most unusual. It's not the way a court properly goes about things, letting people speak out of turn. But if you have no objection, I can see no fault in it. After all, this is an informal hearing, not a formal trial. Mr. Weatherford, you may complete your comments."

But Weatherford was exhausted; he sat in his chair limply and mumbled, "I have said all I have to say, Your Honor. There is nothing more."

"Very well. Please proceed with your argument, Mr. Mapleson."

Mapleson continued. "Mr. Weatherford has correctly perceived that I have closely examined Dr. Jekyll's life, attitudes, and reactions in order to point out Jekyll's complicity in this unfortunate matter of Mr. Hyde. Mr. Weatherford feels that Jekyll's failings are minor. So they might appear to be, but I am arguing that they are not minor because they in fact created Hyde. Hyde was who he was because Jekyll was who he was. I would like to remind the Court of the words of the Lord: 'Alas for you, scribes and Pharisees, you hypocrites! You who are like whitewashed tombs that look handsome on the outside, but inside are full of dead men's bones and every kind of corruption. In the same way you appear to people from the outside like good honest men, but inside you are full of hypocrisy and lawlessness.' Now, if it is true that Hyde is what he is because Jekyll is what he is, it is also true that the original source of the evil lies in Jekyll, not in Hyde."

Judge Freeman interrupted. "Mr. Weatherford, you will recall, also argued that what you said about Jekyll might be construed to apply to the greater part of humanity, to all those who value their reputation in the eyes of their fellow human beings."

Mapleson replied, "If that is the case, then so be it. I am not here to try the human race, but to defend Edward Hyde. If Mr. Weatherford chooses to see in Jekyll a prototype of the general human attitude, I suppose the argument would indeed apply. 'If the shoe fits, put it on.' This conclusion, however, he reached on his own." The Judge seemed satisfied.

Mapleson went on. "Let us now take up the matter of Jekyll's religion. Mr. Utterson told us that before this unfortunate matter of Mr. Hyde, Jekyll had no religious beliefs of any consequence, and that the good works Jekyll performed he did out of a desire to please his fellow human beings, not to please God. However, after Hyde gained power, so Utterson testified, Jekyll became 'sincerely religious' and after the murder of Dr. Carew he attended church: henceforth when he did good deeds, which he now performed more assiduously than ever, he regarded them as done for the sake of the Almighty. So it would appear that Jekyll, out of fear of Hyde, turned to religion, and that though Jekyll once was content with the high esteem of his fellow human beings, he now found it necessary to win favor with God as well.

"This attempt to satisfy God failed, however, and it is important for us to ask why. Several times we learned from Utterson that Jekyll, out of his great distress, prayed to God for help against Hyde. There is not the slightest shred of evidence, however, that God ever helped Jekyll. We cannot help but conjecture that this is because Jekyll's motivation to pray arose from his guilty conscience and his desire to save himself, not out of his love of God. In this, he is much like King Claudius in Shakespeare's play *Hamlet*. You will remember that the guilty king, who murdered his brother to take his throne and marry his wife, prays to God for help but finally concludes of his prayer, 'My words fly up, my thoughts remain below. Words without thoughts never to heaven go.' In fact, if God was watching the struggle between Jekyll and Hyde, it would seem that he not only failed to answer Jekyll's prayers but actively favored Hyde, for in spite of all Jekyll's overtures to the Almighty it was Hyde who gained in strength and Jekyll who became weaker. I submit to the Court that before Hyde is universally condemned for his evil, the Court consider this point: It would appear that, evil though Hyde was, God preferred him to Jekyll. Why would this be so? Because Hyde, however evil, was genuine, whereas Jekyll was a sham. God, we could say, used Hyde to destroy Jekyll because Jekyll's false life was an affront to his Creator."

As Mapleson's argument emerged there was an agitated stir in the courtroom. Weatherford looked even more aghast. Dr. Savant was becoming interested and Ms. Wood leaned forward in her chair as though to catch every word. But it was Dr. Christiansen who sprang to his feet this time, his face red with anger: "YOUR HONOR! I PROTEST! We are here to try Edward Hyde for his crimes, but this man is asking us to judge Henry Jekyll instead. He has alleged that Jekyll's attendance at church, nay, his good deeds themselves, are self-serving, and for this reason his prayer did not reach heaven. No doubt there is an element of self-interest in Jekyll's actions at this desperate point in his life. Who could blame him if there was? But to argue that Jekyll was lacking in sincerity is to point the finger of accusation not only at him but at all those sincere and devout Christians who, in a heartfelt desire to please God, engage in good works and direct their prayers to heaven. If Jekyll be guilty, then so is the greater part of Christendom, nay, those of other religious faiths as well. This in itself is outrageous, but Mapleson does not stop here; he has the gall to assert not only that Jekyll's prayers fail because of his insincerity but that Jekyll created Hyde. I submit, Your Honor, that he has no right to soil the reputation of the devout with such insinuations and should be made to stick to his task of defending Hyde, the one who has truly committed the crimes.

"To make matters worse, Mapleson has introduced the motives of God himself into the argument. He makes much of the fact that God did not answer Jekyll's prayers, and from this he reaches the outrageous and blasphemous conclusion that God favored Hyde over Jekyll and used Hyde to destroy him. It was bad enough to assert that Jekyll was not heard by God because of his lack of sincerity, but to assert that God actively sided with Hyde over Jekyll, and thus gave Hyde the greater energy, is an affront to everything that we know about the goodness and justice of the Almighty. Are we not admonished by Holy Writ to eschew evil and do good? Yet people like Hyde depart from the good and thus embrace an evil that would not exist if they did God's will. Jekyll, however awkwardly, seeks to do good, but it is Hyde, by Mapleson's own admission, who by following only his own will dedicates himself to evil. Surely if God failed to answer Jekyll's prayers it was only to prod his soul on to further devotion: for to imply that God used Hyde's evil for his own purposes is to suggest that God himself partakes of the nature of evil, and we know that this cannot be. Weatherford has pointed out that we are not here to try Jekyll, and I would add that we are not here to try God either!"

Christiansen sat down. The courtroom was stunned by his outburst. Mapleson, who had listened attentively to every word Chritiansen said, began to speak, but Judge Freeman held up his hand for him to wait and, turning to Dr. Savant said, "Sir, we have not yet heard from you, and it would appear to me that since we have heard from Mr. Weatherford and Dr. Christiansen it might benefit the Court if we could now have your opinion. Mr. Mapleson, of course, is not yet through with his presentation, and you will, of course, Mapleson, be allowed to finish, but it might help us to digest what has happened thus far if we had the benefit of your expertise, Dr. Savant, since the argument seems now to hinge on matters of psychological import. For in order to defend Hyde, Mapleson is delving into the psychology of Jekyll, indeed into the psychology of God himself, if we can speak this way of the Almighty."

Albert Savant remained seated in his chair. Thoughtfully he pondered the words he had heard. When he spoke, he addressed his words not to the Judge, nor to Mapleson, but to Dr. Christiansen.

"My dear Dr. Christiansen, it is clear that the points Mr. Mapleson raised upset you. I can understand this, for what he suggests goes against all the conventional and accepted principles of your faith. Your dogma teaches you to trust in the love of God and to believe in God's superior knowledge, insight, intentions, and, above all, goodness. From your point of view, therefore, what Mapleson is suggesting is blasphemous, and the idea that God should do anything other than condemn Hyde is outrageous. In pointing out to us, however, that God operates through and is manifested in Hyde, the counselor for the defense is bringing out an important truth, namely, that God, your theology notwithstanding, is responsible not only for good but also for evil. Now since Mapleson has chosen to introduce God into his defense of Hyde, I think this is an important point. As long as we subscribe to your theology that God can only be and do good, we cannot appreciate the argument the defense is making. There is, moreover, psychological evidence that God, as I have said, originates our promptings toward evil as well as toward good, and it is this evidence that I wish to present before the Court.

"First, however, I must make it clear that when I speak of 'God' I do not refer to the transcendent God of your theology but to the God who appears in the human soul, whom we know as an overpowering impulse from within. For as a psychologist and scientist I can only know what can be experienced. There is a God-image in the human psyche that can be known and experienced and described. We call this the 'Self' since it is a larger personality within us than the ego; it is, in fact, the essential core, the totality and fundamental reality of our human nature that contains the masculine and the feminine, the conscious and the unconscious, in short, all the opposites within us. Please be sure, then, so that there is no misunderstanding, that I am speaking explicitly of this God-image in the soul, for it is quite beyond my knowledge to say anything at all about the God who is the object of your faith. So I would have no quarrel with you except when your theology intrudes on matters of human affairs and psychology, and then I must object when you interject your dogmatic assertions into this sphere.

"What do we know about God from our psychological investigations? We know that he is compounded of opposites. Mr. Mapleson is quite correct, therefore, when he says that God may favor Hyde as much as Jekyll, for God is the totality of everything. He is, you see, both love and its opposite, both the urge to justice and the contrary tendency, both light and darkness, good and evil. Our impulse to good, represented in this case by Jekyll, and our impulse toward evil, manifested in Hyde, both come from God. That is why Mapleson can argue as he does.

"Now as can well be imagined, this duality in God produces a split in human nature, and this split leads directly to the tragedy we are considering today. It is of the utmost importance that we become aware of this split and struggle with it as consciously as possible, for only in this way can we avoid unconsciously identifying with God and therefore with the evil that he embodies. And here, sir, is where you and your theology do humanity an injustice, for when you equate God only with the good and say that evil is not real and would not exist save that people turn away from God's will, you deny the reality of evil. This belittles evil and lulls us into the dangerous illusion that it does not truly exist the way the good truly exists. This attitude lays us human beings open to evil, for, you see, evil has as much reality as good, since the opposites cannot exist save in juxtaposition to each other. Can we think of light without dark, or up without down? Of course not, and neither can we think of good without evil. So when you dogmatically declare that God is goodness and love, that he intends only justice and morality, and that he wants us to eschew evil and do only good, you are encouraging this dangerous split within us. You hope to overcome evil by denying its existence and strengthening our good intentions; but this is not enough, because evil is as fundamental to our nature as good.

"Therefore I must agree with Mr. Mapleson that Jekyll is as responsible for the sad turn of events that we are contemplating as Hyde. For Jekyll, encouraged by such as yourself, has failed in his major task: to become conscious of this split in God and, by means of his consciousness, to heal God's split by uniting the opposites in himself. You see, it is only human consciousness that can hope to resolve the dilemma, and this consciousness must come from human beings, for God is not conscious enough to be moral. God is a blind force. God's consciousness is dim, like a faintly glowing light bulb in a fog. Only human consciousness can be strong enough to see God's dilemma: indeed, without human consciousness the world would only be a gigantic, meaningless machine. God has no foreknowledge of an ulterior goal, nor any clear idea how to reach it. Consequently, though God creates, he makes errors and runs into blind alleys, which accounts for the horrible realities of this life: disease, mutilation, mutations, and the horrors of human conflict. As Creator, God is a force in nature that stumbles and fumbles blindly, creating now this and now that, not with a clear sense of purpose but like a person who rolls the dice to see what will come up. So God, compounded of opposites that struggle blindly against each other, seeks human consciousness for his salvation. In the case of Jekyll and Hyde we see these opposites at work, and Mapleson is correct that Jekyll failed because he wasn't conscious. God could not help Jekyll, for, since he is as much evil as good, he favors Hyde as much as Jekyll, as Mapleson has said. It was Jekyll who had to help God. Only if Jekyll had become conscious of this great split in the divine Nature could he have made the moral choice that would have saved himself and others from the disaster we are discussing. Only as individuals become conscious can humanity escape general unconsciousnesss, and only in this way can God himself be transformed. But you, by denying that evil is as real as good, have made the development of this consciousness impossible."

Dr. Savant had finished. All eyes were now on Christiansen. One would have thought that Christiansen, already disturbed by Mapleson's alarming argument, would be furious or at least shaken by Dr. Savant's devastating remarks. But strangely enough, Christiansen seemed to be in control of himself. "Sir, you say that you are a psychologist, but you speak as a theologian. For is it not up to theologians to speak of God? As far as I am concerned, therefore, what you are expressing are your theological opinions, which, of course, are contrary to the beliefs that I hold from my study of Holy Scripture. I grant you the right to your opinions, for everyone can believe what they like about God; however, I must object to the authoritative way in which you express what you believe. You make pronouncements that do not permit discussion. You accuse me of being dogmatic, but you yourself are dogmatic. Have you some superior access to the knowledge of God? Do you have some way of knowing the Almighty that is not available to the rest of us? No doubt you would say that you base your statements on your knowledge as a psychologist of human nature, though it is not entirely clear how that leads to a knowledge of God. But surely at this point in our human development we are not in a position to claim that we know the depths of human nature. We still 'see through a glass darkly.' You accuse me of being dogmatic, but if I am dogmatic then so are you, with all your talk about what God is like.

"You take me to task because you say I deny the reality of evil. But I didn't say that evil is not real. The Holy Scripture makes it clear that evil is real, and did our Lord himself not deal directly with the Evil One? How can you say that I deny the reality of evil? It is not evil's reality but its origin that I would dispute with you. You say it is from God, I say it is from human deviation from God. You say evil will always be, since it is fundamental to the Creator, and that man must save God from his own evil. I say that evil, springing as it does from a deviation from the divine will, can also be overcome when we are in alignment with the divine will, and that it is God, therefore, who must save man from *his* own evil. Thus I do not deny that evil is real, but I do say that at the core of the universe we find a good, not an evil, being.

"I must point out to you that there is hardly anything original in your position. Save only that you include good and evil in one being, it is as old as the faith of the ancient Persians, who said there was the god of light, Ahura-Mazda, and the god of darkness, Ahriman, in ceaseless opposition to each other. This position, of course, has the advantage of clarity. It resolves paradox and relieves the intellect of its task of answering the question, Why evil if God is good? As for me, I prefer my struggles to your hopelessness, my unanswered questions to your certainty about matters we are not in a position to understand."

Dr. Savant was irritated. "My dear sir, you misunderstand me. It is always the case with you theologians that you fail to listen carefully. Did I not say quite clearly that when I speak of 'God' I do not refer to the transcendent God of your theology, but to the God who appears in the human soul? Did I not make it clear that I was speaking as a psychologist and a scientist and not as a metaphysician? It is not of your metaphysical reality that I speak, but of the 'Self,' the God-image in the psyche. You are therefore free to believe what you like about your God of transcendent reality, for I speak only as a humble empiricist, and none of my statements touches on the nature of the Unknowable. If you had listened to me carefully, you would have heard me say this. As it is, your righteous indignation only adds to the confusion and is entirely misplaced."

It was Christiansens's turn to be irritated. "You must surely be aware of the unfavorable light in which you put me. For you say that the God of whom I speak cannot be known. If this be so, then all statements about God are matters of sheer opinion, since there is no basis for anything that can be called knowledge. With this I do not agree. I do speak of the transcendent God, but I claim that the transcendent God is also immanent in his creation, that he has found ways to reveal himself so that his nature is not entirely unknown. But be that as it may, the fact is, sir, if you were sincere in your desire not to be misunderstood, you would refrain from using the word *God* at all. By long and honored usage this term has been used to refer to Ultimate Reality. If you, then, decide to use the term in another way, you are certain to create confusion. Of course, you can claim the right to use the word *God* in any way you choose—words, as we know, can be defined to mean what we want them to mean. Do this if you like, but do not then be surprised if people misunderstand you. I repeat that, if you are sincere in your desire not to be misunderstood, you will stick to your own language system. Use the word *Self*—it belongs to you, you coined it and defined it to mean what you want—and do not use a system of language that has long been the province of poetry, philosophy, and religion.

"The fact of the matter is, in spite of your protests to the contrary, I believe you do mean to speak of God in the same way that I speak of God. Your statements do not strike the ear like the statements of an empirical scientist but for all the world like the statements of a religionist or, at the least, a philosopher. For example, you say that God is unconscious, a blind Creator who fumbles when he creates and makes mistakes, and as evidence for this you point to the apparent 'mistakes' in nature: to things like disease, mutilation, and mutations. Surely, you are not now speaking only of a God-image in the human soul, but rather of the creative force that moves through the world, the same force that we theologians observe and from which we deduce something of the nature of Ultimate Reality.

The attempt to arrive at a knowledge of God from the nature of creation is as old as Scripture itself; only Scripture sees God's glory, not his supposed mistakes. Does not the psalmist declare, 'I look up at your heavens, made by your fingers, at the moon and stars you set in place—ah, what is man that you should spare a thought for him, the son of man that you should care for him?'

"As for God's supposed mistakes, how do you know what constitutes a mistake? Do you know the divine plan? Are you in a position to decide what has been created correctly and what incorrectly? How do you know that everything has not been created and has not happened exactly as it should? Do you have some superior standpoint? No, my friend, you too are speaking as we theologians speak—only when someone pins you down you cry 'foul!' and say with hurt feelings, 'I am being misunderstood.'

"You say that you are merely a 'humble empiricist.' But I say that if you were truly an empiricist and scientist, as you claim to be, you would offer your opinions as hypotheses. Is not science a matter of hypotheses? Does science ever claim for itself a final answer? Is not the history of science the history of ideas that once were thought to be permanent, inviolable laws and now are known to have been only stepping stones on the way to a still greater understanding of the truth? Scientists today have learned this, and all scientific 'laws' are held to be tentative hypotheses, used as long as they work but ready to be replaced as soon as a more adequate formulation of the truth appears. But you, when you talk of God, use the language of the theologian. You do not say 'It appears at this time as though the Self might be both good and evil.' Instead you proclaim, as some kind of revelation, cast in stone for all time: 'God is . . . God is this and God is that.'

"As for this matter of the 'Self,' for the sake of argument let us accept your language. Let us agree that it is the 'Self' of which you speak and not 'God.' This Self you say is equally good and evil. Therefore its intentions are ambiguous, since it first inspires good in the human ego and then sends promptings for evil. This Self, you say, is our fundamental reality; it is our inescapable and unchangeable human nature. Only the human ego, by becoming conscious of the opposites in the Self, can tip the balance toward a life with some semblance of morality. This, however, implies that the ego has a measure of free will. For if the ego did not have free will, all it could do would be mirror the dichotomy of the Self, being now good and now evil. Well, sir, if you believe in free will, so do I. Only I say that the ego, being left free by God, chooses to deviate from God's will and so creates evil. And this Self—which I agree must exist, for is it not the equivalent of the God within?—is a creative reality, not good in some narrow human sense, but creative, and this creativity is of the very essence of the transcendent God as well. That evil exists in consciousness we both agree, but where you see greed, the lust for power, the hatred we hold for those who oppose us, the cowardly desire to be secure at all costs as promptings of the Self, I see them as the strivings of the ego to protect itself and further its own ambitions instead of obeying God's will."

Dr. Savant was about to reply when Judge Freeman intervened. "Gentlemen! We have listened to your discussion with great interest. I have allowed you to proceed because the counselor for the defense saw fit to introduce God and divine motives into his argument. I think your discussion has been useful thus far, but I fear it will soon veer too far from the matter at hand, for our task is to pass judgment on Edward Hyde, not the God whom you claim to know, Dr. Christiansen, nor the Self you claim to know, Dr. Savant. Therefore I must call a halt to your discussion. But before I ask you to complete your argument, Mr. Mapleson, I think we should hear from Ms. Melanie Wood. Ms Wood, I have observed you. You have sat there quietly, seemingly rapt in thought. A great deal has evidently been going on within you, and this Court must hear it. We have been exposed to a great deal already, however. I therefore declare a recess for one hour. When we convene we will be pleased to hear from you, Ms. Wood, and then ask you, Mr. Mapleson, to conclude your remarks.

# 5 Melanie Wood Speaks and Mapleson Makes His Final Statement

The Court resumed after the hour's delay. The Judge called on Ms. Wood. "Your Honor, I welcome this opportunity to give you my reflections, which will take us in a different direction than the discussions we have had from Mr. Weatherford, Dr. Christiansen, and Dr. Savant. I have listened carefully to the witnesses, to Mr. Dorset, to Mr. Mapleson, and to the stimulating, if inconclusive, discussion between Dr. Christiansen and Dr. Savant. I have only one point to add to what we have already heard. It is a point that I think Mr. Mapleson may also be aware of because of his adroit questions with regard to the marital status of the various participants in our drama: In all this sad story women either played no role, or their role was described in a derogatory way. As Mr. Mapleson's questions have brought out, neither Poole nor Utterson, Enfield nor Lanyon, Jekyll nor Hyde had a wife or any woman as a close companion. Of course not all men are called upon to have a woman for their companion in this life, but when in a group of six men none has a relationship with a woman, we must suspect that something is incomplete.

But that is not all. We do indeed hear of women in this tale of tragedy, but the roles they play would appear to be a sad commentary on my sex. For instance, Mr. Enfield described the women who surrounded Hyde after he had trampled the little girl as 'wild as harpies.' Miss Jones says that she fainted after she witnessed the murder of Dr. Carew, and the Court had to ask her to 'pull herself together' because she was weeping too much. Mr. Hyde's housekeeper was described as an 'evil-faced' old woman. Mr. Poole says that when he and Mr. Utterson returned to Dr. Jekyll's house that last dreadful night one of the maids was 'whimpering hysterically' and had to be reprimanded. When Mr. Poole heard Hyde's lament from inside the laboratory he told us that it sounded 'like a woman or a lost soul'!

"I find myself with certain questions. Why must angry women be described as 'wild as harpies'? The men were also angry when they saw what Hyde had done, but their anger was described as 'righteous indignation.' Miss Jones's inclination to weep during her testimony seemed to disturb people; why is it preferable to discuss such horrors as we have been discussing without any show of emotion? When Mr. Poole returned with Mr. Utterson to his house, he found one of the maids was crying too, but, in his view, it was 'hysterical whimpering.' Perhaps particularly odious is Mr. Poole's comparison of the tortured cry that came from Edward Hyde's damned soul to the lament of a woman. Why must woman's pain be compared to the lament of a lost soul?

"Naturally when I hear talk of this kind I feel that my sex is being disparaged. However, I do not bring up these matters in order to defend my sex. What I wish to point out is that the influence of women on the people involved in this tragedy was absent, ineffective, or negative. I think this fact draws attention, not to the defects of women, but to the defects of the men involved in this matter.

"It means something when men do not relate to women, and it means something when men disparage women and the emotional side of life, which men often leave to women to carry for them. What it says is that the men are undeveloped, that they lack the capacity for intimacy and relationship, and are not at home with their emotions. It means that the men are no longer in touch with those subtle, feeling sensibilities for people and issues out of which compromise and relatedness can develop.

"If Henry Jekyll and Edward Hyde had paid attention to the feminine element in life, perhaps they would have been able to work out a relationship with each other, one that might have mitigated, softened, and transformed the hardened and rigid patterns in which both were set. For as Mr. Mapleson has pointed out, *both* Jekyll *and* Hyde seemed set in concrete. Incapable of change or development, they could only collide with each other to their ultimate mutual destruction. Furthermore, no one else in this whole story was able to do anything helpful for any of the parties involved. We hear of them condemning and criticizing the women, but they themselves were incapable of bringing a positive influence to bear on the situation.

"These thoughts, it may be said, are mere conjectures. But the lack of women in the lives of these men and the unfortunate way in which the women who do appear in our tale are described are facts that point to the omission of one vital half of human nature. In such a case we can expect nothing but tragedy, for the feminine, when rejected, acts like an offended goddess who finds her own ways to take revenge on those who despise and neglect her. Indeed, perhaps without the presence of the feminine quality in life those opposites that Dr. Savant describes so well can only fall into mutual and unending antagonism, leaving the conscious personalities that Dr. Savant says must intervene incapable of the necessary creative responses.

"Does it sound strange to you that I say a goddess might take revenge for neglect of the feminine side of life? Let me remind you of something Dr. Savant said: that the Self, as he called the core of our being, is both masculine and feminine. To carry his thought a bit further, since he compared the Self to God, we could say that God is both masculine and feminine. Now God, according to Dr. Christiansen, is concerned with justice, and justice is what we are concerned with in this courtroom. Justice is usually considered from the point of view of laws and the breaking of laws, and punishment is meted out in accordance with penalties that are prescribed in advance according to the importance of the law that has been broken. This idea of justice—a fixed penalty for breaking a fixed law—might be called masculine justice. However, if Dr. Savant is correct, there must also be feminine justice, and this feminine justice would operate differently. Feminine justice treats each case individually; it is never the same twice, for it is specific to a certain person, a certain relationship, a certain situation. It operates especially when there is a matter of love, rejection and relationship. It is, if you like, capricious, but it is not mindless; it is irrational, but not pointless; unpredictable, but not unintelligent; as natural as nature herself, but not ineffective.

"Yet I fear that it is exactly this feminine justice that is being overlooked in the case at hand. Consider, for instance, the matter of the 'harpies.' Mr. Enfield spoke disparagingly of the women who were 'angry as harpies,' and no one offered to defend them. Well, suppose they were angry as harpies; who were the harpies? They were the ancient Erinyes, or Furies, of the Greeks, defenders of the laws of nature, of all natural blood ties among human beings, powers who presided over what was right and correct in life and took terrible vengeance on those mortals who disregarded the laws of relationships that govern human life and the natural order. If the women did act as harpies, it tells us that a feminine power is deeply concerned that a terrible offense has been committed against the underlying laws of natural life. These women are, then, not to be disparaged, but seen as the agents through which divine fury is expressed.

"I say to you, Your Honor, that feminine justice has acted in this case. Hyde, of course, has been punished by his death and universal condemnation. But Jekyll died too, and Mr. Mapleson seems to be suggesting that he merits our condemnation as much as Hyde. Oh, we may exonerate him in terms of masculine law, as Mr. Weatherford did when he pointed out that Jekyll broke no laws of society: but insofar as Jekyll failed in relationship, avoided his own truth, and sinned against the laws of nature herself in creating the personality of Edward Hyde, he brought down on himself the other law of which I speak: the dreadful law of the feminine and the punishment of the Erinyes.

"Would Dr. Christiansen agree with me? Dr. Christiansen talks of God and of God's justice, but he thinks of God in masculine terms. I agree with what he says of God's justice, but I think of God also in feminine terms. I say that God was offended by the human beings in this sorry story and meted out justice accordingly. We limit God's justice because we think of God as masculine. Do we not refer to the Divine as he? By so doing we fail to see the full extent of the divine justice that falls on us when we offend the natural laws of life, and it is this justice that we see at work in the case of Henry Jekyll and Edward Hyde."

Melanie Wood was finished. The courtroom was hushed. The Judge looked thoughtful, then spoke: "Ms. Wood, I must say your comments have taken our deliberations in a new direction. Yours is not the usual point of view that we hear in this Court. I am, of course, trained in the matter of justice, deeply steeped in matters of English and Roman law and its history. But yours is an entirely new way of looking at the matter of justice, law, and just retribution. It would be fitting if we took the time to discuss these matters at more length. However, I will have to ask Mr. Mapleson to do this for us, since time presses upon us, and he must be allowed to complete his argument. Mr. Mapleson, please resume your case."

Mapleson had listened intently to Christiansen and Savant, but especially to Melanie Wood. He began, "Your Honor, and ladies and gentlemen, I want to express my appreciation to Ms. Wood. It is true, as Ms. Wood has inferred from my questions, that I have been impressed by the lack of women in the lives of the men involved in this tragic matter. However, she has gone beyond my reflections, and her remarks have helped me clarify thoughts that were not yet clear to me, thoughts that I find important to my final argument.

"First, I emphasize the importance of Ms. Wood's comments that the presence of a feminine quality might have mitigated, softened, and transformed the hard and rigid patterns in which Henry Jekyll and Edward Hyde were set. I think the matter goes even further, and this same quality might, if it had been present, have been the bond, the cement to join together these two halves into a whole. That the two are meant to be one being is surely proved by the fact that neither could let the other alone, that each was in his own way dependent on the other, and that when Jekyll died so also Hyde died. How else could the warfare between them have ended unless the goddess of love herself had whispered her words of peace and understanding into the ear of each offended, fearful, enraged half of a man?

"Second, I wish to comment on the remarks made by Dr. Christiansen and Dr. Savant, especially what they have said about God—or the Self, to use the word Dr. Savant prefers. Ordinarily matters of theological or psychological import have no place in a trial. In this case, however, as I hope to make clear, the relationship between whatever divine Being may exist to the participants in the crimes we are considering is important. I ask you, therefore, to bear with me as I reflect on the statements of Dr. Savant and Dr. Christiansen and then proceed to make my own position clear.

"Dr. Savant understood me to say that God favored Hyde as much as he did Jekyll because God is good *and* evil and therefore sends urges to do both good and evil into human consciousness. He sees the case we are considering as a substantiation of his point of view: that good and evil alternate, that both are equally strong in the 'Self,' and that Jekyll expressed the good side of this Self and Hyde the evil side.

However, this is not my position. I do not say that God used Hyde for an evil purpose, but that God used Hyde's evil for a divine purpose. When *I* speak of evil I mean that power that destroys what is whole and sound. This does not mean that God does not have a dark side, but a careful distinction must be made betwen the dark side of God and evil. The dark side of God is indeed terrible to behold, which is why Holy Writ warns us that 'it is a terrible thing to fall into the hands of the living God.' But the dark side of God destroys that which is not fit to exist, whereas evil destroys that which *is* fit to exist. If our state of being—our consciousness, if you like—is not what it ought to be and is not fit to exist in God's eyes, then we can expect to encounter God's dark side, and we will deem it evil since it aims at our destruction. God, I am saying, does not will evil into being but can use even evil for the purposes that his dark side requires be carried out.

"There is a biblical precedent for this point of view, found in the saga of Joseph in the Book of Genesis. You will recall that Joseph was imprisoned by his jealous brothers and thrown into a pit. They intended to murder him, but when some Ishmaelite traders came by on their way to Egypt, they sold him as a slave instead. That was as good as killing him: however, it so happened that Joseph did not die as a slave but, because God favored him, he became the prime minister of Egypt and saved Egypt from famine. Eventually, because of this famine, all of Joseph's family also came to Egypt, and in this way his brothers came under his power. Joseph protected them and treated them kindly. Nonetheless, when Jacob, their father, died, the brothers feared again for their lives, saying that now their father was dead Joseph would revenge himself on them. But Joseph reassured them, and with reference to their plans to kill him, he said to them, 'You intended it for evil, but God used it for good.'

"This point is important for my case, for I am arguing that Hyde's great vitality, and his evident power to destroy Jekyll, shows that God used him to destroy a personality that was, in God's eyes, not fit to endure. If this is correct, in God's eyes Jekyll was a greater evil than Hyde."

Judge Freeman listened intently. Dr. Savant appeared irritated. Weatherford still looked stunned by the whole proceeding. Ms. Wood's attention was fixed on Mapleson. Dr. Christiansen looked perplexed, but interested, at this unexpected use of Scripture.

Mapleson continued: "But neither can I agree with Dr. Christiansen's point of view. Dr. Christiansen is shocked at my sug-

gestion that God used Hyde, evil as he was, for divine purposes. He would like to believe that God is above such things,
that God dwells in a realm of love and apparent goodness that
makes it unthinkable that he would have anything to do with
evil. He says quite explicitly that to believe that God actively
sided with Hyde against Jekyll is an affront to everything
known about the goodness and justice of God. Dr. Christiansen
also said that he derives much of his knowledge from Holy
Scripture. Scripture certainly speaks of the love of God. But
does it not also talk about the wrath of God? Does it not admonish us to 'fear' God—which would only be appropriate if
there was something frightening about the divine? Indeed, to
repeat what I just said, Scripture states that it is a terrible thing
to fall into the hands of the living God. Is God loving? We
hope so. Is he terrible? Certainly. Is God to be loved? I believe
so. To be feared? Beyond a doubt. For this God is dark and destructive, no 'White Giant' guaranteeing our security and con-
soling us in our self-created difficulties, but a Deity who is a
creator and therefore destroys that in creation which is not as it
should be.

"Does not a writer who composes a faulty sentence tear it out
ruthlessly and write another? So perhaps God tears out from
his creation that which has become faulty and makes another
attempt. And never is this more necessary than in the realm of
human life, for here God's creatures are capable of deviating
from the divine will and choosing a path they are not meant to
follow.

"Or so it would appear. For who can say what God is like? We
have heard much today about the supposed nature of God. Dr.
Christiansen says 'God is this' and 'God is that.' And Dr. Savant
also says 'God is this' and 'God is that.' But who knows what
God is? Who can claim to have plumbed the depths of the Almighty and to be capable of making such pronouncements? So
I do not say 'God is' but only 'it appears that God may be acting
this way in this case.' But I remind the Court that if there is a
reasonable doubt that an accused person is not guilty of the

crime of which he is accused, he must be acquitted. Edward Hyde has been accused of being the most heinous of all persons, and the sole instigator of evil in this case. I argue that because of the evidence that God may have favored Hyde over Jekyll, Hyde, though certainly not innocent, is not as guilty as charged.

"It may be asked, What then of Dr. Danvers Carew, whom Hyde also killed? Was his life also so imperfect that God saw fit to destroy it? Of course the human mind cannot comprehend all the injustices of this world. Of one thing we may be sure: the innocent also suffer. Perhaps the suffering of the innocent is the price to be paid for a world in which spiritual development can take place. So it was, at least, in the Bible, for did not the innocent children of Bethlehem suffer when Christ was born?

"We may also ask, What kind of justice is this if God uses the evil of Hyde to destroy a person whose life has not won favor in his eyes? It is, surely, a justice of a different kind than the justice meted out by this Court, for Jekyll, as Mr. Weatherford has reminded us, is not guilty of breaking any of the rules of society. But Ms. Wood pointed out that there is another kind of justice. She calls it feminine justice. This justice does not obey fixed rules. It is individual and particular to the circumstances of each situation. It is free to select whatever line of action, whatever punishment, is exactly appropriate, and it operates whenever the right, natural, and harmonious order of things has been violated. Now I have hitherto referred to God as 'he.' I did this because the use of the masculine pronoun is conventionally accepted and makes discussion simpler. But at this point we do well to speak of the Deity as 'she,' for the kind of justice we are discussing seems to partake of the qualities of feminine justice that Ms. Wood described. God's justice in this case, Ms. Wood suggested, is more like that of a goddess who is personally and deeply offended than of a God who sees that a law has been broken.

"I submit to you, ladies and gentlemen, that what we see in

this case is the judgment of God, and that this judgment fell more on Henry Jekyll than it did on Edward Hyde. This is why Hyde's energy increased and Jekyll's decreased. If God, in his infinite, divine wisdom, perceived Hyde to be the lesser evil, who are we to heap the guilt only on him?

"This may sound like a harsh judgment on Henry Jekyll. Mr. Weatherford believed that when he realized what I was saying. He felt that if Jekyll was thus to be judged, so was the greater part of humanity. For in what respect do those among us—a majority perhaps—who seek the respect and honor of their fellows differ from Henry Jekyll? Dr. Christiansen was also shocked, and reminded us of the biblical admonition to eschew evil and do good. Yet, does history not show that many people who sought the favor of their fellows perpetrated great horrors? In times of war and persecution do not those who persecute and destroy others win the praise of their fellows?

"So I argue that Jekyll's evil, though more subtle, is responsible for Hyde's evil. If I am correct, Hyde is Jekyll's creation. If Jekyll had not been what he was, Hyde would not have been the evil person he proved to be. To be sure, seen from the outside, Jekyll appeared good enough; but all his seemingly good actions were done for the sake of his dear and glorious ego, and this engendered the evil. I might add that how a person such as Jekyll might have saved God from himself, as Dr. Savant implies he should have done, escapes my comprehension. The result of Jekyll's falseness was the accumulation of evil on the inside, in the manner pointed out by the Lord when he spoke of the Pharisees being like whitewashed tombs that look fine on the outside but inside are full of dead men's bones.

"Your Honor, I thank you for your patience. I hope you can understand why I had to proceed in this case as I did. I will now summarize my argument as succinctly as I can and then rest my case: Hyde has been falsely accused of being the author of all the evil in the tragedies we have considered because he is himself the creation of Jekyll. Jekyll is the greater evil, and I offer as proof that the divine power favored Hyde over Jekyll, refusing to answer Jekyll's prayers and giving Hyde the greater energy, thus aiding in Jekyll's final destruction. Hyde, therefore, is to be condemned for his crimes but not for his existence. The greater judgment, which history has hitherto placed on Hyde, should fall instead on Jekyll. With this, I rest my case."

Mapleson slumped down in his seat, limp from his exertions. A ripple went through the courtroom—of anger, thoughtfulness, amazement, even anguish. For several moments Judge Freeman was lost in thought. Then he rose and rapped his gavel. "Ladies and gentlemen," he declared, "I had expected to render speedy judgment in this case; however, the argument has taken an unexpected turn, and it is worthy of my careful deliberation. This court therefore is adjourned until four o'clock."

# 6  The Judge Reaches a Verdict

It was 4:00 P.M. The courtroom filled rapidly; there was not an empty seat in the gallery. The witnesses were in their places: the nervous Miss Jones, the impassive Poole, the timid Enfield, the trustworthy Utterson. The panel of experts was ready: Dr. Christiansen, alert and attentive; Dr. Savant, comtemplative; Mr. Weatherford, still looking troubled; Ms. Wood, rapt with interest. District Attorney Dorset sat at his table with his aides. He radiated confidence, yet in his eyes there was just a hint of doubt. Counselor Mapleson looked tired and drawn.

The door to the Judge's private chambers opened. The clerk entered, and Judge Freeman followed him. The Judge strode to the bench, rapped unnecessarily for silence, and declared, "This Court is now in session."

He spoke: "Ladies and gentlemen, we have deliberated on whether the judgment passed on Edward Hyde by history, that he was guilty of heinous crimes and is to be universally condemned, was fair and just. At the beginning of this hearing there was little doubt in the minds of most of us, I am sure, that Edward Hyde was indeed guilty, and that it was right that he be universally condemned for the evil he perpetrated. It was only to satisfy the complete demands of justice that this hearing was granted at the request of Mr. Mapleson.

"We have heard the witnesses. Mr. Enfield testified that he saw Hyde trample an innocent little girl; Miss Jones said she saw Hyde murder the elderly Dr. Carew; Mr. Poole informed us that in his opinion Hyde destroyed his master, the eminent Dr. Henry Jekyll; and Mr. Utterson corroborated all this testimony. District Attorney Dorset has argued, drawing on the testimony of these witnesses, that Hyde is indeed guilty of these crimes and deserves the unilateral judgment the generations have made upon him. When Counselor Mapleson chose not to cross-examine these witnesses, challenging neither their veracity nor the facts they presented, it appeared that no defense of Edward Hyde was conceivable or possible.

"However, Mr. Mapleson did offer a defense—an unusual defense, if I may say so. He has argued that though Edward Hyde is guilty of crimes, he does not deserve the one-sided judgment placed on him for two reasons: first, because Hyde, Mapleson alleges, is the product of the false life and false personality of Henry Jekyll and, therefore Jekyll's is the greater evil; second, because God himself favored Hyde over Jekyll and used Hyde for his own purposes, showing thereby that in God's eyes Jekyll's evil was greater than Hyde's. So, Mapleson argued, if this is God's judgment, who are we to judge differently?

"Our four experts responded vigorously to Mapleson's argument. Mr. Weatherford expressed strong disapproval. If Jekyll was evil, so he informed us, the greater part of humanity is equally evil, for do not all respectable people seek, like Jekyll, to win the respect and favor of their fellow human beings? Dr. Savant expressed appreciation for Mapleson's argument, saying that God, or the Self, as he prefers to call the Divine, is both good and evil and was equally manifested in Jekyll and Hyde. Mapleson, however, it should be noted, said that Dr. Savant misunderstood him. Dr. Christiansen was shocked at Mapleson's argument, for, notwithstanding Mapleson's quotation from Genesis—'You meant it for evil, but God used it for good'—Dr. Christiansen could not accept the thought that God, whom he sees as devoted to love and justice, would use the evil Edward Hyde as his instrument. Ms. Wood, however, pointed out that there are different kinds of justice. There is masculine justice, she said, which operates by law, and feminine justice, which operates from nature, and Mapleson, utilizing her insight, declared that the justice God brought about in the matter of Jekyll and Hyde was this same feminine justice of which Ms. Wood spoke.

"Such is the argument for the defense, and I am impressed by it. Mr. Mapleson has, I must confess, come up with an original defense of Edward Hyde, one that I could never have foreseen. I must commend him for his able presentation. There were times when I feared he was toying with this Court, but in fairness to him I now see that he had a serious defense to make.

"However, his argument is not beyond criticism, for it rests only partly on facts, and the remainder is a matter of opinion about matters that can only be regarded as uncertain. It is, for instance, a fact that Hyde grew stronger and Jekyll grew weaker and that finally Hyde quite destroyed Jekyll, and Mapleson brought this out clearly. But is it also a fact that it was *God* who favored Hyde?—*God* who gave Hyde the added strength and even *intended* Hyde's ultimate victory? Dr. Savant and Dr. Christiansen, both of whom have justifiable claims to know something about these matters, both deny this. For Dr. Savant says that God, being equally evil and good, would not favor one over the other, nor would he have any unified purpose. Dr. Christiansen says that it is unthinkable that a God of goodness and love could ever favor a man like Edward Hyde. In an area where even such experts as these disagree, can we regard Mr. Mapleson's argument as anything more than opinion?

"Now, it is also a fact that Henry Jekyll was something less than genuine. No one, not even his good friend Mr. Utterson, denies that Dr. Jekyll was overzealous in currying the favor of his fellows and went to great lengths to make a good impression on others. But is it also a fact that the falseness of Jekyll's personality actually created Hyde? Not even Dr. Savant, who is an expert in such matters, reached this conclusion.

"I have pondered these issues deeply, for it seems that what Mapleson is asking us to do is reach a conclusion that has great implications. He has asked us to pass judgment, not just on Edward Hyde, whose crimes he does not defend, but also on Henry Jekyll. Now, as Mr. Weatherford has pointed out, this amounts to a judgment on virtually the whole of humanity. For if Jekyll is guilty because he in effect produced Hyde, who among us can claim to be free of guilt?

"Mapleson's argument also challenges our cherished ideas of God. We have been confronted, in fact, during these proceedings with three ideas of God. Dr. Savant would have us believe that God is equally good and evil and is too unconscious to reconcile these opposites within himself; therefore they are represented in common humanity, producing now a Jekyll and now a Hyde. Jekyll, he tells us, is to blame, as Mapleson has said, but not for Mapleson's reason; he is to blame because he failed to become sufficiently conscious to hold the opposites in God, whom Dr. Savant prefers to call the Self, in some kind of balance. But if Dr. Savant is correct, what hope can there be for humanity? Can the unaided human ego, without the benefit of divine grace, which apparently does not exist, or if it does exist must be forever balanced by divine malevolence, ever save itself?

"Dr. Christiansen, on the other hand, tells us that God is good and loving and just, and therefore would never stoop so low as to use Hyde for his purposes, much less favor him in a struggle against Jekyll. Yet Mapleson has argued that God, though not in himself (or herself, as the case may be) evil, can and does use evil for his own inscrutable purposes. That is indeed a cornerstone of Mapleson's defense, for, so he says, if God preferred Hyde, who, however evil, was at least genuine, to Jekyll, who, however good he seemed to be, was in fact a fraud, then who are we to place all the blame on the defendant in this case?

"Where there is such marked disagreement even among experts, we must assume either that we do not possess enough facts or that the implications of those facts are not clearly understood. I find that I am not capable of determining who among the many voices we have heard is correct. Therefore I have decided to render a judgment based on what is known, or at least generally assumed, and not try to exceed the limitations of a court of justice. For I am a judge and cannot claim knowledge of the divine will. The justice that I dispense is the justice codified in the laws of society. According to these laws, murder, assault of one person on another, and a conspiracy on the part of one person to destroy another are crimes. Of these crimes Edward Hyde is manifestly guilty, indeed, he is a particularly malignant example of offenses against all that society holds dear. Henry Jekyll, on the other hand, is not guilty of any actions designated by society as a crime; he may be guilty of certain moral failures, even, as Dr. Savant has pointed out, of having failed to reach the proper level of consciousness, but for these things, though God may pass judgment upon him, this Court cannot.

"For this reason my final ruling is that I uphold the universal condemnation of humanity against Edward Hyde. I deem him guilty as commonly regarded and worthy of the condemnation against him. To do anything less would be to condone, and perhaps encourage, others to likewise commit such crimes. Therefore, as a judge, called upon by my society to uphold the laws of the land, I accept the arguments of Mr. Dorset and reject those of Mr. Mapleson.

"However, I am also a private person. As a man I will carry Mr. Mapleson's words and arguments in my heart. There may well be a feminine justice that God carries out. It may be that God destroys that which is morally and psychologically weak and false, even using that which is evil for this purpose. It may be that those of us who resemble Henry Jekyll are indeed responsible for those who are like Edward Hyde. I contemplate these questions that Mapleson has raised, and am reminded that each of us lives not only under the laws of our society but also under divine law, that divine law and human law may not necessarily coincide, and that we may be adversely judged by God even when we are innocent in the eyes of human law.

"Ultimately God's authority is greater than that of this Court. Though human law tries to hold down and punish evil, uprooting it when it can be seen, the way a gardener pulls the weeds from a garden, it knows little of the seeds of the evil that it thus seeks to destroy. We seek to destroy the manifestations of evil, but perhaps God seeks to destroy evil itself. Each of us then must carry away the awareness that the seeds of evil may be in ourselves. Edward Hyde thus stands condemned, but we do not go free from our own guilt or responsibility.

"Ladies and gentlemen, this Court is now adjourned."

Judge Freeman departed through his private door. As the Judge left the room, Enfield, Poole, Miss Jones, and Utterson disappeared—vanished into thin air. The people in the gallery rose to depart, at first in silence, then beginning to talk in low, hushed tones as they went out through the doors at the back of the room. Mr. Weatherford was the next to leave; he walked alone, an unhappy look on his face. Christiansen and Savant followed him, walking together and talking with each other earnestly. Dorset nodded goodbye to his aides and then went over to Mapleson and extended his hand.

"No hard feelings, I hope. I was only doing my job, you know."

"I know," said Mapleson, standing and taking the proferred hand. "It's all right."

Dorset left. Only Mapleson and Melanie Wood remained.

"Ms. Wood—" Mapleson began.

"Why don't you just call me Melanie? It would be easier."

"Yes. Thank you. Melanie, it's been strenuous, don't you think?"

"I quite agree, Mr. Mapleson."

"I would like it if you called me Andrew."

"Of course, Andrew."

"I thought the Judge made a good speech, didn't you?"

"Yes. But aren't you disappointed that he did not decide in your favor?"

"No, not really. You see, I didn't expect that he would. How could he disregard the laws of society for which he stands? Besides, I'm not even sure of these things myself. I'm a counselor for the defense. I argue as best I can for my client. But I can't always be sure."

"You mean you didn't believe what you were arguing? I

thought what you said was most impressive. Do you think perhaps Dorset or Dr. Christiansen or Dr. Savant is right?"

"No, I don't think they are right, not entirely right, at least. But I'm not sure I'm right either—about God, that is. As I said before, people are always saying 'God is this' or 'God is that.' So Christiansen says 'God is good and just,' and Dr. Savant says 'God is good and evil' and 'God is too unconscious to be moral.' But how can any human being assume that he knows all this about God?"

"Dr. Savant seems to know. What most people call God, of course, he calls the Self, though, of course, he talks of God when he wants to."

"Call it God, call it the Self, I don't think any of us can claim a final knowledge. How would anyone know? Is any of us in full possession of the facts at the core of the universe? or the human psyche, for that matter? Can any of us claim for ourselves a private revelation that gives us final and complete knowledge of these matters? I think in his own way Judge Freeman reached this same conclusion. I am satisfied. He at least heard the argument, and looked at the issues, and had the grace to urge us all to do the same."

"I suppose you are right, and that it was the best for which you could hope. But what do you really think about evil? Dr. Savant says it comes from God, but Christiansen says it comes when people refuse to follow God's will."

"Who really knows? Maybe it has many different causes. Like cancer. I'm told there are over a hundred different types of cancer, and many different reasons for them. Just the same, cancer always manifests itself as a disease that gradually destroys the wholeness—call it the goodness, if you like—of the body. Maybe evil is like that—something with different causes, but that, no matter what the cause, destroys the goodness of the soul unless it's stopped."

"Judge Freeman and others like him try to stop it by punishing it."

"The outer manifestations of evil can be punished, but that won't stop it from cropping up again. If I'm right and Jekyll was worse than Hyde, what human law can punish him? We just saw Judge Freeman decline to do so. No, I fear human law cannot prevent evil from coming up again and again. It helps, but it doesn't stop evil, because the causes of evil are deep."

Ms. Wood spoke again: "You know, it's said that the body has its resistance to cancer, that our immune system kills off cancer cells—in fact, is doing so all the time. Maybe it's that way with the soul. Maybe the soul can also destroy the urge to evil when it appears."

"Yes, maybe it can, but, like the body, it must be healthy to do so. And Jekyll's soul wasn't healthy because of the kind of person he had become."

"And how do you have a healthy soul?"

"I think all our souls are healthy when we're born. It's a problem of keeping the soul healthy. I suppose it's done by seeing yourself for what you are, acknowledging your own evil when it crops up and not making someone else carry it for you, and being connected to other people whom you care about. That's where you come in. You were a big help, you know."

"I was?"

"Yes, with your point about feminine justice. I knew there was something there but hadn't quite figured it out."

"I'm glad I could help."

"Melanie?"

"Yes?"

"It's getting late. I'm famished. Haven't been able to eat very much, with the tension of the trial. Would you have dinner with me tonight? I hate to eat alone."

"Well. . . . I had plans, you see, . . . but I think I can change them. Yes, Andrew, I would like that."

Moments later Andrew and Melanie left the room arm in arm, talking animatedly. The courtroom was silent and empty as the doors closed behind them.

# II COMMENTARY

# 7 Introduction

Religion without a thorough study of sin, religion without awareness of conscious and unconscious, individual and collective darkness, evil and deviation, is not religion but blind idolatry.
—FRITZ KUNKEL

Any discussion of the problem of evil must make certain distinctions; otherwise it will fall into a quicksand of confusion about difficult and emotion-laden issues. One basic distinction that must be made is between natural evil and moral or psychological evil. Natural evil refers to events such as earthquakes, floods, pestilence, or disease. These events we regard as evil because of the seemingly senseless suffering they inflict on us. The fact that many people who suffer from natural calamities do not in any way deserve it (e.g., children who are born into the world with birth defects) only adds to the problem we face in explaining a world in which such evil events take place.

Natural evil also includes the dangerous side of the archetypes. Though a study of the archetypes would take us beyond the scope of this book, we do need to note that each archetype has a light and dark, a positive and negative side. If a person is heedless of the nature of the archetype, or has a negative relationship to the archetype, the dark side of that archetype is experienced. The archetypes are the psychic natural world in the human being. Like all nature, there is a dark and dangerous side that a person must keep in mind. If you go into the wilderness and are careless, you may pay for it with your life; in the same way we cannot ignore our own archetypal psychology without running into its dangerous side.

Moral or psychological evil, however, is different from natural evil, for moral or psychological evil refers to the evil things people do to each other and themselves. This kind of evil originates in the human psyche and includes varieties of criminal behavior, the atrocities of war, and all the various forms of inhumanity and cruelty that members of the human race so often inflict on each other.

It is difficult for people who believe a good God created the world to account for the existence of natural evil. One argument has always been that those who suffer deserve it. Like Job, I personally reject this argument and lay the blame on God, not human beings. Although I can conceive of situations in which people might in some sense deserve the suffering inflicted on them by natural evil, I can also see many situations in which those who suffer do not deserve it. Like Job, I call God to account for the kind of creation he has made and agree with Isaiah's understanding of God when he wrote, "I [God] form the light, and create darkness: I make peace, and create evil: I the Lord do all these things" (Isa. 45:7, KJV).

This Old Testament picture of God can be called unflinching monotheism: God is responsible for the world he has created, and its evil as well as good is laid at God's door. However, though in the Old Testament in many places God is said to be the author of natural evil, he is not the author of psychological or moral evil. To the contrary, God is consistently represented by the prophets and others as calling on human beings to do justice and practice mercy, and he deplores the moral depravity of human nature as an aberration from the divine will. When Isaiah quoted the Lord as the creator of evil it is natural evil, not psychological evil, of which he speaks.

It is to the question of moral or psychological evil that this commentary is addressed. What is the psychological origin of our tendency to do inhumane things to each other? What does the existence of this propensity toward evil in people say about our fundamental human nature? Does the existence of psychological evil have implications for our understanding of the nature of God, and if so, what are they?

These are deep and difficult questions that require careful, thoughtful answers. In order to focus on these issues I am deliberately not exploring perspectives on the general problem of evil offered, for instance, by Eastern philosophy. And although there will be frequent references to the implications of our ideas about evil for our ideas about God, the main focus of this book is psychological, not theological. The main questions before us concern the origins of evil in the human psyche.

But before we go on to these questions, we must ask a more philosophical but no less important question: Is there any valid way to determine what is good and what is evil? Indeed, is there moral evil at all, or is this idea only an invention of the human mind?

It might seem as though the answers to these questions are obvious. Don't we say instinctively of other people or events that they are good or evil? Aren't we constantly passing judgments of this kind? It is true that we are, but it is also true that different people arrive at different judgments, so that what one person deems to be good another person may deem to be evil. To take one example, a few years before the Pilgrims arrived in New England a terrible plague all but destroyed the local Native American population. Historians speculate that smallpox or measles had been spread among the Indians by a slave ship that happened to touch on the New England coast, and that the Indians, with no natural immunity to the strange European diseases, as a consequence died by the thousands. When the Pilgrims found the land filled with corpses and bones but empty of living inhabitants, they deemed it a great good, and various Puritan divines preached sermons praising God for his goodness in clearing the land of the savages and making it available to the new people of God. The Puritans deemed the plague a great good, but no one bothered to interview the Indians. If someone had, we can be sure they would have called it a great evil.

Similarly, in time of war when one side wins a victory it is called a good, but the other side regards it as an evil; of course, both sides believe God wants them to win. Leaders of opposing nations at war are also thought of differently. Adolf Hitler was a glorious leader for most of the Germans prior to and during most of World War II, but he was a symbol of evil for much of the rest of the world.

It is clear that our determinations of what is good and what is evil vary greatly, and one person's value judgment may contradict another's. This is because such determinations of good and evil come from the ego. What suits the purposes of one person's ego is called good and what goes against it is called evil, whereas from the point of view of another person's ego exactly the opposite judgment may be made. Moreover, the more egocentric a person is, the more distorted that person's judgments of good and evil become. This is what led Hamlet to declare to Rosencrantz, "There is nothing either good or bad, but thinking makes it so."[1]

This egocentric determination of good and evil comes out clearly in the attitudes of Henry Jekyll and Edward Hyde toward each other, for each one regards the other as evil. Jekyll wanted to rid himself of Hyde (after he felt Hyde's destructive powers turned on himself), and Hyde wanted to destroy Jekyll because of personal animosity toward him.

If the egocentric point of view was the only way people arrived at judgments of good and evil, we would have to conclude that there is no such thing as genuine morality and no sound basis for the human conscience. We would also have to conclude that the universe in which we live is amoral and, therefore, that life is fundamentally meaningless.

Fortunately, however, not all determinations of good and evil are made from the ego, for C. G. Jung has shown that the feeling function arrives at conclusions of value apart from the machinations of the ego.

One of the many important contributions of Jung to psychology is his typology. Most of us are familiar with his terms *extravert* and *introvert*; we understand them to mean that some people are oriented primarily to the outer world and some to the inner world. But in addition to these two primary modes of orientation, Jung said there are four psychological functions by means of which the ego becomes aware of information and arrives at conclusions. He called these four functions thinking, feeling, sensation, and intuition.

Jung's typology has found a life of its own, and many people today know about his four functions of the psyche who know little about the rest of his psychology. Partly this is because of the practical applications of this part of Jungian psychology. The nature of the four functions is so well known it is not necessary to discuss them further here. The one that is important to us now is the feeling function, because Jung argued that it is through the feeling function that people arrive at value judgments. For instance, when we look at a situation and say, "This is terrible!" or "This is good," we may be placing a value on that situation via the feeling function, and not simply looking at it from the point of view of the ego. And if we conclude that a certain individual is a good or bad person, it may likewise be a feeling judgment and not an egocentric judgment.

Certain people have the feeling function as their primary function, and these people typically have a heightened awareness of the values of life. For this reason they are often people-oriented and may also have a heightened social conscience. However, the feeling function is part of each of us, and when it is active it gives us a sense of value independent of the ego.

An interesting example of the feeling function comes from the annals of World War II. It is because of the feeling function of one man that the city of Paris is intact today when so many cities of Europe were destroyed. Toward the end of the war, when Eisenhower's armies were moving toward Germany and the fall of Paris was imminent, Hitler sent to command the garrison at Paris a general who was an expert in destruction. Gen. Dietrich von Choltitz had been in charge of the scorched-earth policy in the Soviet Union; as the German armies retreated von Choltitz saw to the destruction of every bridge, road, house, and living animal that might in any way help the approaching Russian armies. Von Choltitz seemed to be just the man to carry out the task Hitler had in mind: the complete destruction of Paris.

General von Choltitz arrived in Paris intending to carry out orders as usual, but he slowly came to change his mind. He was a military man. It made military sense to him to carry out the scorched-earth policy in the Soviet Union, but it made no military sense to him to destroy Paris. So he stalled. Days, weeks went by, and von Choltitz found one excuse after another for postponing the destruction of the city. Pressure from Hitler's headquarters mounted steadily, but von Choltitz felt more and more strongly that the destruction of Paris was wrong. Eventually he realized that the only hope for saving Paris was the capture of the city by Eisenhower. Eisenhower did not regard Paris as an important military target, however. One Allied army was driving south of the city and another north of the city, and Eisenhower figured Paris would simply fall into the bag. But von Choltitz knew that by that time he would have been replaced (executed, no doubt) and the city destroyed. In desperation he implored a Swedish businessman who happened to be in the city (Sweden was neutral during the war, if selling ball-bearings and iron ore to the Germans can be called neutrality) to get through to Eisenhower and beg him to move directly on Paris. The Swedish gentleman got through, and Eisenhower acted, sending the Fourth U.S. Infantry Division and a Free French armored division with orders to advance directly to the rescue. When the Americans and the French arrived, von Choltitz drew up his garrison, marched out of the city, and made a fight of it. He was no traitor to his country! He lost, of course, managing to get himself captured, fortunately, and the Americans and the French marched triumphantly into an unscathed Paris.

This is an instance in which a man acted in a way that was counter to his ego's seeming best interest. In fact, he risked disgrace and life itself in acting as he did. He acted from his feeling function, and it gave him a sense of value that was not founded on egocentric desires. There can be no doubt that the feeling function is one of the bases of a healthy human conscience.

The feeling function in the story of Jekyll and Hyde appears in Mr. Utterson. Throughout the tale, as his witness in *The Strange Trial of Mr Hyde* makes clear, Utterson was repelled by the evil that he saw in both Hyde and his friend Jekyll. Utterson gives us a human, redeeming point of view, because as a feeling person he could transcend his egocentricity and thus arrive at an objective evaluation of what is good and what is evil.

Helpful though it is in freeing our sense of right and wrong from the tyranny of the ego, the feeling function is not always a reliable guide, because it must operate on the information it has at its disposal. If we could always see situations completely in all their meaning, we might always arrive at valid value judgments through the feeling function. But what if our information or our conscious perspective is incomplete? Or even incorrect? Then our feeling function, healthy enough in itself, might still err, simply because it was misinformed about the facts.

The Koran tells the story of Moses and the angel Khidr. They are traveling together when they come upon a fishing village. Khidr, seemingly out of pure malice, sinks all the villagers' boats, and Moses is horrified and complains about it. Khidr explains that, unknown to Moses, robbers were on their way to the village to steal their boats. If Khidr had not sunk them, the robbers would have taken them; as it is, all the villagers have to do now is raise them up again and repair them. In another incident Khidr falls upon a young man and brutally kills him. Again Moses is horrified and objects, but Khidr tells him that this young man was going to murder his father and mother that evening and, if he had done so, his soul would have been condemned to hell forever. By killing the youth Khidr saved the parents from death and the young man from everlasting damnation. In these tales, Moses' feeling function filled him with a sense of horror and moral repulsion at the acts of Khidr, but when he understood why the angel acted as he did his value judgment changed.

One of the results of the process of becoming whole that Jung called individuation is that we come to see the overall pattern of our lives. This leads to a certain kind of wisdom and a conscious perspective that helps us see many things in a different light. As a result our value judgments change. In the trial Mapleson understands enough of this to be led to quote Joseph, from the Book of Genesis. Joseph was the victim of his brothers, who intended to murder him but instead sold him as a slave, since that was as effective as killing him but would not bring blood vengeance on them. Joseph, however, did not die as a slave and eventually became the prime minister of Egypt. When famine came to that part of the world, Joseph's brothers had to come to him in Egypt for food. Joseph welcomed them, forgave them, and provided a home in Egypt for them and their aging father, Jacob. But when Jacob died the brothers were fearful that Joseph would now take revenge on them. Joseph knew their anxiety and tried to reassure them. Referring to their plot against him, Joseph said:

"The evil you planned to do me has by God's design been turned to good." (Jerusalem Bible, Gen. 50:20)

or

"You meant evil against me; but God meant it for good." (RSV)

or

"But as for you, ye thought evil against me; but God meant it unto good." (KJV)

Joseph's brothers certainly did intend evil when they planned to murder Joseph and then sold him as a slave, and at that time Joseph would no doubt have agreed that this was a purely evil event. Only much later, after Joseph had matured and was prime minister of Egypt and had saved the people from starvation, did he see that, though the brothers' plot was evil, God had used it for good. In his mature life Joseph's consciousness had greatly expanded, and he understood that God can use evil for a larger purpose.

Not only does Joseph's remarkable statement hint at the paradoxical purposes of God for allowing evil to operate in the world, it also shows us that if our evaluation of good and evil is to be sound our feeling function must be operative and our consciousness must be expanded. Only if we transcend the narrow viewpoint of our egocentric egos can we begin to come to terms with the larger issues of the problem of evil.

A Joseph-like perspective embodies the perspective of the Self and differs from that of the ego. In fact, what the ego calls evil may be deemed good from the point of view of a higher consciousness. When things are looked at from the point of view of heaven they look different than they do when looked at from a purely earthly point of view.

We are now in a position to comment on the true basis of conscience. By conscience we understand that faculty within us that gives us a sense of right and wrong, and an urge to do the right. Most of us are aware of the "voice of conscience" within us, but if we probe deeply enough we may find that what poses as conscience turns out to be the introduced (internalized) opinions of our parents, our church, or other authority figures. Freud called this the superego, by which he meant the internalized collective opinions and attitudes of the society in which we live. In Jungian psychology, these collective opinions are often expressed by the negative animus (in the case of a woman) or negative anima (in the case of a man). The result is that we may be misled about the true right or wrong of a situation. We may then become neurotic as we are induced to act contrary to our deepest, though unconscious, convictions and feelings. In such a way a false conscience leads to evil, not good.

The true basis of conscience is not collective opinion but the Self, which, from the religious point of view, is like the will of God within us. Out of our inmost Center comes the instinct for right and wrong, and the urge to do that which is right, even if this conflicts with collective expectations. It is also out of the Self that there comes the capacity for love that is fundamental to the truly moral life. When we are cut off from the Self, our instinct for moral action is weakened, and instead of the Self we find ourselves following the dictates of others which may or may not coincide with our inmost truth. Nevertheless, the Self is always there, even if hidden from us, acting like a vital power trying to bring us back to our moral center. It is more powerful and deeper than the ego. When the ego departs from the Self, the unconscious sets up an opposition to the ego. To live a moral and correct life is to live in accordance with the Self. To go against this deepest Center within us is to incur the enmity of the Self. The morality of the Self may be different from the collective morality in which we are immersed in our social structure. The morality of the Self emerges in our awareness only as we grow in consciousness; thus the growth of individual consciousness and individual morality go hand in hand.

In the trial, Mapleson introduces the point of view of the Self in his analysis of the relationship of God to Jekyll, on the one hand, and God to Hyde, on the other. This will become clear later on when we discuss the relationship among the ego, the persona, the shadow, and the Self. But for now we must confront the question, Is it true that there is a Self within us that can be trusted as a moral guide? Is it true that there is a Self at all? The answers will depend to a great extent on how we answer another question, From whence comes moral or psychological evil? It is to this that we now turn.

NOTES:

Epigraph: Fritz Kunkel, *Selected Writings*, John A. Sanford, ed. (New York: Paulist Press, 1984), p. 256.
1. William Shakespeare, *Hamlet*, act 2, scene 2, line 259.

# 8 Psychology and the Origin of Evil

Our answer to the question of the origin of psychological evil will necessarily influence our worldview. By a worldview is meant how we see ourselves in relationship to this universe in which we live. For instance, is life a meaningless accident with no inherent purpose? Is it, as Macbeth said, "a tale told by an idiot, full of sound and fury, signifying nothing"?[1] Or is there some ultimate purpose to life, some unseen and meaningful factor at work amid the apparently senseless confusion of human existence? If so, what is the relationship of this tiny speck of life that we call our personality to that ultimate purpose? Do we live in a universe that is unaware of and uncaring about our existence? Or is there in creation a reality that in some sense "cares," a larger meaning to which we somehow belong? At death does the flicker of life in us disappear like the flickering flame of a candle when it is snuffed out? Or is there no death, as Chief Seattle once said, but "only a change of worlds"?[2]

Insofar as psychology strives to be a pure science it will say that these questions do not concern it, because they are metaphysical questions and do not fall within the purview of science. For science must concern itself with what can be experienced and known; it cannot be burdened with the task of supplying answers to scientifically unanswerable questions about our place in the universe. This task is left to religion, which is free to deal with metaphysical questions in any way that it chooses, not being limited by the strict empiricism of the scientific method.

On the other hand, psychology's offspring, psychotherapy, cannot entirely avoid these questions. For psychotherapy seeks the healing of the individual personality, and both the thoughtful ego and the soul ask questions about the ultimate meaning of life. Especially as we get older, our psychological health may depend on how we answer the question of our place in the universe. And even if, on the level of the ego, we do not concern ourselves with these religious issues, the soul does concern itself, and is restless until the ultimate questions of life are dealt with in a meaningful way. Consequently psychology, insofar as it involves the practice of psychotherapy, comes up against religious issues whether it wants to or not. Thus psychology and religion, which the intellect might like to regard as entirely separate and distinct, each with its own concerns and methodology, meet each other when individual human beings try to find meaning for themselves. Since the soul is intrinsically religious, that is, concerned with the ultimate meaning of things, psychology must at least look at the religious issues of life. Religion cannot afford to ignore psychology either, for the understanding of human nature held by any particular psychological viewpoint will inevitably have implications for our worldview, as we will see.

Nowhere is this interrelationship of psychology and religion more apparent than in the answers given by psychology to the question of the origin of moral evil. The way we answer this question will inevitably influence our religious attitude.

We will begin with the answers of secular psychology to our question. By secular psychology I mean a psychology that denies that there is any other center to the personality than the ego. A secular psychology would deny the existence of anything we might call soul. It would also deny the existence of anything like a divine influence at work in human personality, since that would amount to another center at work within us in addition to the ego. According to secular psychology, human life and existence must be understood only in existential and personal terms, and the ultimate reference point is always that of the ego. If there is such a thing as a divine power in the universe, it has nothing to do with the workings of the human mind.

The psychology of Sigmund Freud is an example. Freud said that at birth we are a bundle of instincts, which he termed the id. These instincts seek fulfillment. They are not guided or regulated by any inner center, but strive blindly to fulfill their particular inner urges. They are bound to be destructive to organized society unless the individual is socialized through a process of cultural education and the ego becomes sufficiently strong to control the instincts and give them a certain amount of rational guidance. Since the unconscious is intent only on satisfying its blind, innate needs, there is no inherent meaning to personality.

Furthermore, one of these instincts is the "death instinct." The death instinct gives birth to the "death wish," the opposite of the id, which is basically a life force. As the name implies, the death instinct draws us back to death. It might be the driving force behind suicide or other self-destructive behavior. It might also be expressed outwardly in aggression, criminal behavior, or war. The worst of human evils can be traced back to this instinct and the wish for death and destruction that accompanies it. Since this instinct, like all instincts, is innate and fundamental to human nature, Freud's outlook on life is pessimistic.

The only hope Freud offers is that we can become conscious of these hitherto unconscious drives. If we become aware of them, we may be able to make rational and conscious choices and decisions rather than be driven by irrational, unconscious forces. The psychologically enlightened ego can perhaps prevent instinctual life from expressing itself destructively without having to resort to repression, with the neurotic consequences that repression entails. It is up to the ego to make an uneasy compromise among the demands of the instincts for gratification, the requirements of the social order, and the need to avoid repression of instinctual life and its consequence, neurosis. The therapeutic goal of psychoanalysis is thus to make conscious the instinctual life and to strengthen the ego in dealing with it rationally. No help from within can be expected to assist the ego in this task, since there are no spiritual forces or centralizing tendencies in human personality to give such help.

It's clear that, if Freud's understanding of personality is correct, the answers to our religious questions must be that there is no divine influence on or within the psyche. Neither is there any goal toward which our inner life is striving. As a consequence, we must accept that life is a cosmic accident without inherent meaning. Freud drew the logical conclusion: Religion and belief in God are illusions to be outgrown if we wish to become mature people. As for evil, it's a "just-so" story. It's just a fact with no meaning, and requiring no explanation, that the instinctual life of human beings has an innate tendency toward the destructive behavior that we call evil.

Another secular psychology that has been especially influential in academic circles is behaviorism. Behaviorism rejects the method of direct introspection as a way of acquiring psychological knowledge; it says that knowledge of human nature must come solely from observation of behavior. In fact, for most behaviorists there is no mind to study, there is only behavior. We *are* behavior.

According to this view, behavior in human life is influenced just as it is in animal life: by conditioned response and reinforcement. Animals tend to repeat those actions that bring satisfaction and pleasure and avoid those actions that bring pain, and human beings do the same. The behaviorist recognizes no difference between human beings and other animals except that human beings, being higher on the evolutionary scale than other forms of animal life, have more complex behavior patterns. Thus people are what they have been conditioned to be. They can be changed by being re-educated, through operant conditioning and positive reinforcement, to behave in different, more desirable ways. There is no mind, and there is no soul. As for evil, it has no objective existence but is only a human category. There is nothing inherently good or evil; there is only behavior that is deemed by society desirable or undesirable.

As we have seen, Freud said that human development is mostly influenced by our instinctual life. We are healthy when our instincts are as completely expressed as society and its requirements permit. We become neurotic when they are repressed. Behaviorism says that it's not instinct that determines the kind of personality we become, but the kind of conditioning to which we have been exposed.

There is a third type of secular psychology that says the important thing is neither instinct nor conditioning, but the kind of early relationships we had as children. According to this view, it is the interaction among people that is the determining factor. Especially important in shaping our later development is the kind of interaction that takes place between the child and significant adults. When these early relationships are favorable and nourishing, the child grows into a healthy adult; when these early relationships are destructive, the seed is sown for an adult personality that is ill, distorted, or even evil.[3]

The best-known representative of this point of view today is perhaps Alice Miller, who has argued in her several books that early life experiences significantly influence our later development. Miller believes that the tendency of human beings toward criminal behavior or destructive actions is not innate but is a reaction to negative childhood experiences and relationships. The mistreated child becomes the distorted and perhaps even evil adult. Miller believes that the Freudian hypothesis that the death instinct is responsible for hatred and human destructiveness stands in the way of seeing the truth: that destructive behavior comes as a reaction to the way people treat each other. To support her argument Miller discusses the lives of some well-known people, treating them as case histories. One of these is Adolf Hitler. Miller makes an impressive argument that Hitler's evil life was the result of his extreme mistreatment as a child, his destructiveness the result of long pent-up hatred, especially for his brutal father. For Miller, evil is thus a reactive, not innate, phenomenon.

Perhaps because she does not believe human beings are born

evil, Alice Miller is able to offer a ray of hope for the human situation and to avoid the extreme pessimism of Freud. She believes that once people know the truth, and understand how their destructive behavior is affecting their children, they will change. We are the victims of false teaching on how to raise our children. Once the influence of the false pedagogy that has dominated parents for so long has been dissipated by being exposed to the truth, evil will no longer have power over us.

The conclusion to be drawn from such a psychology is that if we had a perfect childhood we would be free of a tendency toward evil. On the other hand, if we had a destructive childhood we would be virtually compelled to become evil.

Alice Miller's works have contributed a great deal to psychology and psychotherapy. Many thousands of people have been made more aware of the significance of the early years of their life for their later development. Her cogent analyses of the lives of various people demonstrate the importance of early childhood relationships. Nevertheless, it also appears evident that people with positive childhood experiences are still capable of evil later in life. It also works the other way around: Some people are capable of living decent lives even though they had terrible experiences as children. There seems to be something within us, something fundamental to our human nature, that gives to us a certain amount of free will and enables us to overcome even the most adverse life circumstances. This is a point with which Alice Miller herself seems to agree, for at the end of her book *For Your Own Good* she declares, "For the human soul is virtually indestructible, and its ability to rise from the ashes remains as long as the body draws breath."[4]

Another psychological point of view that deserves mention here, to which we will return later, is that of the Zurich analyst Adolph Guggenbuhl. Although Guggenbuhl did not attempt a general theory of why people do evil, he did make an interesting and searching analysis of the psychology of the psychopath, that person who seems to lack a conscience or sense of right or wrong of any kind. The conclusion that Guggenbuhl reached in his book *Eros on Crutches* is that the capacity for eros is fundamental to moral behavior.[5] He regards morality as a collectively sanctioned model of conduct that is socially useful, but he sees the fundamental source of a truly moral life as eros and the capacity that it gives to a person to relate to and care for others. He believes that as far as love is concerned the psychopath is an invalid because he or she is constitutionally incapable of eros. Because these people lack eros, they live immoral lives without compunction and do evil without guilt. This incapacity to love is not the result of destructive childhood influences but a fundamental lack in their psyche. It is a sort of moral birth defect that leaves the psychopath incurably defective in the area of love and hence unable to live a life that takes the feelings of others into account. Unconnected to other human beings because of their lack of eros, such people can apparently commit the most heinous crimes without a qualm of remorse or conscience.

Before concluding our thoughts on the contribution of secular psychology to a study of the origin of moral evil, let's return to the point Alice Miller made in *For Your Own Good* that the human soul is indestructible. Although Miller doesn't tell us just what she has in mind when she speaks of the soul, it is clear that it is not identical with the ego. This leads us to the idea that there might be a fundamental aspect of our personalities that is not the ego but acts like another center within us. C. G. Jung and Fritz Kunkel believed that the psyche does indeed have another center in addition to that center of consciousness that we call the ego: they called this other center the Self, or, in Kunkel's case, the Real Self or Center.

Both Jung and Kunkel believed that though the ego can be damaged by destructive early influences the Self cannot. We can compare the relationship of ego to Self to the relationship of a piano to music. A piano can be damaged, or even destroyed, but the music the piano is designed to play cannot ever be damaged or destroyed. Music exists in the archetypal realm and therefore is safe from the evil that human beings can do. For this reason Kunkel believed that the Self can help us overcome even the most negative conditions and adverse circumstances.

As we have seen, secular psychologies argue convincingly that destructive early childhood influences, the wrong kind of early conditioning, and innate instinctual tendencies toward evil profoundly influence the kind of people we become. But if there is a second center to personality, as Jung and Kunkel assert, then the matter is more complicated. It is to this type of psychology, which we can call a religious psychology, that we now turn.

## NOTES

1. William Shakespeare, *Macbeth*, act 5, scene 5, lines 26–27.
2. T. C. McLuhan, *Touch the Earth* (New York: E.P. Dutton, 1971), p. 30.
3. Freud also believed early childhood experiences were influential, but he saw their importance in terms of the frustration and denial of instinct. For the school of thought we are now considering, it is the relationship among people that is important, that is, how they treat each other.\4.       A l i c e Miller, *For Your Own Good* (New York: Farrar, Straus and Giroux, 1983), p. 279.
4. Adolph Guggenbuhl, *Eros on Crutches* (Dallas: Spring Publications, 1980).

# 9 C. G. Jung and the Problem of Evil

As we have seen, C. G. Jung and Fritz Kunkel differ from secular psychologists because they posit the existence of two centers to the personality instead of one. For them, the ego is the center of the conscious personality, and the Self is the center of the total personality. The Self is the larger reality that includes the ego and the unconscious. The Self can be likened to the circumference of a circle that includes within it all that belongs to us. It can also be compared to the center of the circle, and is for this reason sometimes referred to by Kunkel as the Center or the Real Self in contrast to the ego, which is the center of a smaller part of our personality. As the larger personality within us, the Self is the source of the energy and strength of the ego. The Self also initiates the striving toward wholeness that Jung and Kunkel called individuation. Without a relationship with the Self, the ego is devoid of vital energy, creativity, and a sense of meaning in life. On the other hand, the ego is also of vital importance to the Self, for if the potentiality of the Self is to be realized, it must be expressed through the life the ego lives. Thus ego and Self are meant to have a relationship in which each supports and serves the other.[1] This relationship can be represented in the diagram on page 98.

The belief that there are two centers to personality is what gives a religious quality to the psychologies of C. G. Jung and Fritz Kunkel. When I speak of a religious quality I do not mean that any theological beliefs or creeds are involved. The religious quality is ego's acknowledgment of a greater psychic reality than itself; namely, the Self. This enables personality to be reorganized around a larger center than the ego. For this to

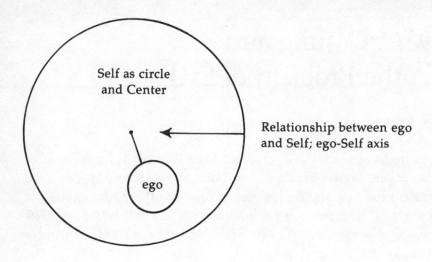

Self as circle
and Center

Relationship between ego
and Self; ego-Self axis

ego

happen, a certain attitude must develop in the ego that bears the hallmark of the religious. The ego must be willing to submit to what amounts to something like the will of God within the personality. It must religiously devote itself to trying to understand and follow the guidance and unfolding patterns that come from the Self. It must understand that its life is no longer its own but belongs to a greater reality. It is thus not a matter of metaphysical beliefs with which we are concerned but of psychological or spiritual attitudes that must necessarily accompany, and emerge from, the individuation process.

It is interesting to note that Christianity also says there are two centers to personality. The existence of the ego is assumed in the Gospels, because people have free will and moral responsibility. The other center is referred to by Jesus in the Synoptic Gospels as the kingdom of God (or kingdom of heaven). (In the epistles it is called the Christ within). Though the kingdom of God has an outer reference, it also has an inner reference, as is clear from Jesus' sayings, such as Luke 17:21, "Behold, the kingdom of God is within you" (KJV).[2] St. Paul also clearly refers to the two centers of personality when he says in Galatians 2:20: "I live now not with my own life but with the life of Christ who lives in me."

If there are two centers to personality, we are confronted with the question, From which of these centers does evil arise? The ego has fantasies and impulses to do evil, and all too often these fantasies and impulses culminate in evil actions. Do the impulses toward evil originate in the ego or in the Self?

Jung wrestled with this question and returned to the problem of evil many times in his writings. Unfortunately his statements are often confusing, because he seldom stops to define his terms. For instance, he frequently says that the Self is both light and dark. But is this darkness of the Self to be equated with evil? As we will see later, if something is dark, even destructive, it is not necessarily evil. Night is also dark, but we think of the darkness of night not as evil but as a welcome relief to the light of the day (how unbearable life would be if it were light all the time!).

Neither does Jung define what he means by good or evil. When he speaks of goodness he often seems to have in mind perfection or purity. A person who is good, therefore, would be pure, with no element of the dark quality, no paradoxes to his or her other nature—a being without blemish, in short, without a shadow. Such a person would be a childlike obeyer of the rules, someone who never had a sinful thought or temptation. Quite correctly, Jung points out that a person who strives to fulfill such an ideal is going to be only half a person. That person will lose touch with the shadow and lack vitality and humanness. Unless the dark side is included, a person cannot be whole.

I don't know of any serious thinker who would quarrel with Jung's analysis that a good person by this definition is one-sided and unreal and will have repressed the dark side of his or her personality. This is not, however, the idea of goodness that Jesus had in mind when he said, "Be ye therefore perfect." The Greek word inadequately translated "perfect" is the word *teleios*, which means "complete" or "brought to an end state." In short, Jesus is urging us to become individuated, just as Jung does. Nor is this the idea of goodness Jesus had in mind when he rebuked Simon the Pharisee. Jesus was being entertained by

Simon when a woman who had led a sinful life came into the house and, weeping copiously, washed Jesus' feet with her tears and dried them with her hair. Simon was shocked that Jesus would have anything to do with a woman who had such a bad reputation. Jesus, knowing his thoughts, reminded him, "It is the man who is forgiven little who shows little love" (Luke 7:47). Clearly, for Jesus, what makes for a good person, and a person who is able to love, is a paradoxical matter.

Not only does Jung not clarify his terms, he often gives contradictory answers or opinions. As we will soon see, Jung ascribes evil as well as good to God. Yet at the end of his autobiography Jung says that the essence of God is an indescribable love. He goes on to quote St. Paul from 1 Corinthians 13, after which he says, "These words say all there is to be said; nothing can be added to them."[3] Because of this confusion, it is not easy to know exactly what Jung thought about the relationship of evil to the Self. It is even possible that he thought different things at different times. However, there is one place in which he deliberately and definitively directed his attention to the problem of evil and its relationship to the Self. This is his book *Answer to Job*, a book that has also greatly influenced subsequent Jungians. It is to this that we now turn.

Jung wrote *Answer to Job* in the spring of 1951, ten years before his death. He tells us in his *Letters* that he wrote the book in a burst of inspiration during an illness, that it was like being seized by the spirit, and that the experience of writing the book was like "landing the great whale."[4] In his letters Jung has far more to say about *Job* than about any other book that he wrote. In spite of the controversy the book aroused Jung never modified or retracted the position that he took in this book; in fact, he expressly said that it was the one book he never wanted to rewrite. Therefore, although Jung made other statements about evil that could be seen as contradicting or modifying those in *Job*, I think we are safe in taking this book as his definitive position on the matter. It seems clear that Jung himself intended this.

Using the Book of Job in the Old Testament as his starting point, Jung proceeds in *Answer to Job* to attack the prevailing canonical image of God and replace it with one that he feels is better supported by psychological experience and the Bible itself. God in the Book of Job, Jung asserts, is tyrannical and overpowering. He appears as an overwhelming but blind force. He never answers Job's just plea for an explanation for his misfortune but tries to overwhelm Job by his power. Job, Jung says, is morally superior to God, for God, though infinitely more powerful than the frail human being Job, is a blind force that is too unconscious to be moral. Therefore, God has the power, but morality and consciousness have to be supplied by Job. Translating this into psychological language, the ego has the capacity for morality and consciousness, whereas the Self is a blind and amoral force.

Also, Jung suggests that God's dark side (which he considers is evil) is revealed in his unjust treatment of Job. This evil side of God was revealed in the image of Satan, who in the beginning of the Book of Job tempted God to afflict the innocent Job with a series of disasters.

Jung says that this evil side of God was never integrated into the Christian canonical God-image. The specific failure of Christianity is its failure to include the evil side of God in its understanding of the divine nature. For this reason there is a split in the Christian God-image. This split emerges clearly in the final book of the Bible, the Book of Revelation, in which Christ and Antichrist, whom Jung sees as the two unreconciled halves of God, are engaged in a final and apocalyptic struggle for supremacy.

God, according to Jung, needs to be healed of this split. For this purpose he sought to become incarnated in human beings in order that his opposites might unite with the aid of human consciousness. This incarnation of God was begun in Christ but was not completed, because only God's light and good side was accepted.

The full incarnation of God therefore remains a task for the human ego to accomplish. This task is nothing less than the realization in consciousness by the human ego of the light and dark, good and evil sides of God. This does not mean we are to do evil, but that we are to become conscious of the urge to evil in all of its divine depths and dimensions.

It is essential for both God and humanity that this be done. If God is to be saved from his own split it must come about through the psychological awareness of the human ego. On the other hand this process is also necessary for the survival of humanity. For if we do not identify and become aware of the archetypal evil in God's nature, we will identify with it and succumb to it. The dark side of the Self will express itself through us the more it goes unrecognized, and then disaster will result. The two world wars, the holocaust, Auschwitz and Dachau are examples of the breaking out of the archetypal evil in the Self. Now that human beings have atomic weapons, we can only expect something much worse in the future. Only the ego's awareness that these opposites exist within its own inner core—the Self, from which comes our image of God—can stem the tide of evil.

The answer Jung gives to the question of the origin of human evil, therefore, is that it comes from the Self. God is to be feared precisely because he fills us with evil as well as with good. To be sure, there is the matter of the ego's personal shadow, but it is of minor importance. The great danger comes from the archetypal shadow, that is, from God's evil. Negative social conditioning and unfavorable childhoods fail to explain the depths of evil of which a human being is capable. Adolf Hitler may have been injured as a child, but such abysmal evil as he perpetrated came because he identified with the evil side of the Self. To be sure, early childhood injuries may be the door through which evil enters, but the evil itself is archetypal (divine), and that is why it is so destructive. The true danger comes from beyond the ego. This is Jung's point of view, and it is expressed by Dr. Savant in *The Strange Trial of Mr Hyde*.

It can be seen that Jung turns Christian theology upside

down. Evil comes from God, not from human beings, hence there can be no doctrine of sin. Instead of sin we have unconsciousness. The incarnation takes place for God's sake, not humanity's, for it is God who needs redemption from his internal split. The human ego is the redeeming agent, for only the ego has the capacity for consciousness and morality necessary to perceive and safely contain God's opposites. What hope there is for the condition in which humanity finds itself must come from the possibility that the human ego can accomplish this awesome task.

Now all of this sounds like theology, and theology is what theologians talk about. It is not surprising, therefore, that theologians such as Philp and Buber took exception to *Answer to Job*. Psychology is concerned with the nature of the human psyche, and theology with answers to the ultimate questions of life. The word Self, as Jung uses it, is a word with exclusively psychological meaning, but the word God commonly refers to the transcendant as well as immanent reality that is the Ultimate Author of life and its meaning. Of course, Jung said in his introduction to *Answer to Job* that he is using the word God in a special, psychological sense. Nevertheless the word resonates within us with overtones of meaning that have metaphysical and theological import. It is understandably hard when one reads Jung to keep in mind that when he says God he does not mean what the rest of the world means when it speaks of God. Although Jung complains bitterly in his *Letters* and elsewhere that the theologians misunderstand him, his choice of language is calculated to bring about exactly this kind of misunderstanding. In the trial, Christiansen points this out to Savant. He objects so strenuously to what Savant is saying because he can't help but take Savant's statements as referring to the ultimate nature of the universe. And for Christiansen, theologian that he is, it is unthinkable that at the heart of the universe there should be an amoral deity who is half good and half evil.

As we have already noted, in his introduction to *Answer to Job* Jung explicitly denies that he is talking theology or making statements that have a metaphysical reference. He claims he is only discussing the canonical image of God in the Bible and its psychological referent, the Self. In spite of this disclaimer, it is easy to get the impression that Jung *is* discussing theology after all, that is, that he really believes the God-image he is portraying in *Answer to Job* not just refers to the Self but also corresponds to the way Ultimate Reality is actually structured. One suspects that he has in mind a new conception of God to replace the old one, that he is not discussing the archetype of the Self but the "creator of the world," to use the phrase he uses in at least one place in *Job*.[5] One also gets this impression when he argues that the notion of God as a conscious being is a prejudice that has led to disastrous conclusions and urges instead a new conception of God that acknowleges the divine unconsciousness and lack of reflection. Jung feels that this would allow us to accept the idea of God's unreconciled opposites of good and evil.

There are also certain of Jung's letters in which he comments on *Answer to Job* that strongly suggest that the God he had in mind when he wrote the book is indeed the creator of the world and the same God theologians have in mind. For Jung seems to have a kind of natural theology; that is, he argues from the nature of creation to the nature of God. He writes, for instance, "The innermost self of every man and animal, of plants and crystals, is God."[6] And elsewhere he says, "Without me it is only his [God's] almighty will, a frightful fatality even in its grace, void of sight and hearing, void of knowledge for precisely that reason. I go together with it, an immensely weighty milligram without which God had made his world in vain."[7]

There is plenty of evidence for Jung's thesis that evil is an essential and ineradicable part of the human psyche; it is not necessary to resort to discussions with theological overtones in order to defend the idea. Murderous orgies, callous trafficking in drugs, the death camps of Nazi Germany, and a host of other ghastly atrocities committed by human beings against each other find a ready explanation in the notion that human beings are simply inherently evil. When we look at a murder committed by a person who had no personal involvement with the victim, who committed the crime coldly and without passion, who did not murder on impulse or out of a sense of being wronged but in a deliberate and detached way, it is not hard to reach the conclusion that the motivation comes from the collective unconscious. This means that evil is archetypal, and thus an inevitable and ineradicable part of our human makeup. This conclusion is very much like Freud's conclusion, only Freud spoke of the death instinct instead of the collective unconscious. But in either case it is a way of saying that people do evil because they are evil, and no amount of therapy, religion, operant conditioning, exhortation, or moral education will change this. Leopards don't change their spots, as the saying goes. This is the seemingly obvious, basically simple, and apparent answer to the question, Whence evil in human nature? It shocks our moral sensibilities, but it can be said that it satisfies all the intellectual requirements. Jung could easily have argued for this position on the basis of psychological facts without using language with theological overtones.

Jung's conclusion that human beings are innately evil as well as good is an arguable position, but it is harder to support his belief that the only beings in this universe that have consciousness are human beings. We have already seen that in many places in *Answer to Job* and in his *Letters* Jung asserts that God is unconscious, that without a human being the world would only be a meaningless machine, created in vain by a deity who is void of sight or hearing and who is dependent on the ego of human beings to supply awareness in the world. Even if we understand that by saying God we mean the Self, it would be hard to comprehend how anyone could know such things. How can we be sure human beings are the only conscious entities in a creation of which we know virtually nothing? How can we be sure that the Self lacks awareness? How can we be sure that God lacks awareness?

Robert May, in his book *Cosmic Consciousness Revisited*, points out that Jung denies the validity of mystical experiences.[8] According to May, Jung, who is often accused of being a mystic, actually equates so-called mystical experiences with an emptying of consciousness from the ego so that the ego is absorbed into the unconscious. For Jung, this means a lowering and loss of consciousness, since, for him, only the ego can have consciousness. Experiences with what Eastern, Christian, and Zen mystics would call God-consciousness or cosmic consciousness Jung would call a consciousness that may be vast but is dim. Mystics, on the other hand, claim that in their experiences of God their consciousness is both definite and acutely heightened. The mystics of the world, through their experiences, would seem to contradict Jung's thesis that only the ego has consciousness and to posit the existence of a consciousness that far transcends the ego in its scope.

In at least one place in *Answer to Job*, however, Jung clearly departed from his analysis of the biblical God-image and ventured into the realm of theology. This was in his attack on the theological doctrine of the *privatio boni*. The doctrine of the *privatio boni* is an attempt to account for the existence of evil without either saying that God is the origin of it (as Jung is saying) or falling back on a form of dualism (as the Gnostics did who said there was a god of evil and a god of good). To come up with a theory of the origin of evil that does not fall into either of these camps is like walking a tightrope, but many Christian thinkers from Origen and Augustine through Thomas Aquinas have made the attempt.

The basic idea of the doctrine of the *privatio boni* is that evil came about when the creation fell away from the perfection God intended for it. Evil is thus the "privation" (diminution) of the good. The reality of evil consists in the fact that something is not what it is meant to be. If it was what it was meant to be, it would be whole and sound and good. Evil is thus like a "mutilation of the soul" (Basil of Caesarea), a distortion of something created sound into something unsound.

On the level of psychological evil this is a way of saying that evil enters into consciousness when the ego departs from what it is meant to be. This condition is always possible, because God permits the ego to have free will. Without free will there would be no morality, no choice, or even any true love of God. The price of free will is that human beings may choose to depart from their true natures, and when this happens there is a distortion in personality that results in evil. Looked at in this way it might be more accurate to say that evil is not a falling away from the good but a betrayal of the good.[9]

Jung was bitterly opposed to this doctrine because he believed it denied the reality of evil. In denying evil, he believed it also encouraged evil. He asserted that the doctrine paved the way for people to ignore evil and therefore fall victim to it. His strong reaction was based on his negative feeling about what he took to be the consequences of the teaching. He also believed it was illogical and called it a "nonsensical doctrine."[10] He never spoke of the doctrine of the *privatio boni* except in the most critical, even sarcastic tones.

However, the fact is that, though the doctrine denies that evil is ultimate, it does not deny evil's reality. Put philosophically, it says that though evil is real, only the good has substance. This is a way of saying that only the good can exist in its own right, but it does not deny evil's reality. Thus evil cannot create on its own; it can only attack that which is created. This is why Origen and Augustine could say that, in the end, when God's plan is complete, evil will cease to exist, because it is not ultimate. When creation is fulfilled there will be no evil, but for now evil is very real indeed, a fact to which the Gospels clearly bear witness, as we have seen. Many of these points are argued by Christiansen in his debate with Savant.[11]

Jung's *Answer to Job* has won wide acclaim. It has performed a valuable service for many people who, like Job, have been victims of an evil for which they were not responsible. It is a helpful compensation for the tendency of Christian theology, and many modern psychologies as well, to place too heavy a burden on the human ego. It also helps us overcome what one analyst called our "infantile religious attitudes often stemming from saccharine childhood training."[12] It cures us of any notion that we may have had that God is to be loved but not feared. Indeed, so powerful is the book that for many it has become a veritable bible of Jungian thought. For example, Jungian analyst Edward Edinger places it alongside the sacred scriptures of the world in value and asserts that it gives the world a "new myth" to replace the old, faded myths that no longer are able to help us.[13] But, as we will see, not everyone reacted to the ideas in *Answer to Job* so favorably.

## NOTES

1. Certain contemporary Freudians like Kohut and Winnicott also use the term Self, but in a different sense than Jung and Kunkel use it. For Jung and Kunkel the Self has an *a priori* existence and the ego emerges from it. For Kohut and Winnicott and others, the Self is gradually built up as the ego assembles, so to speak, the various aspects of the personality. It could be said that this leads to a "sense of oneself," that is, one's identity as a person. Though the idea of a Self of any kind is an innovation in Freudian theory, its importance is far less than in Jungian psychology.
2. See my book *The Kingdom Within* (San Francisco: Harper & Row, 1987), p. 33. Luke 17:21 can also be translated "among" you. The Greek preposition *entos* implies both within and among, which is a way of saying that the Center lies both within us and among our relationships with others.
3. C. G. Jung, *Memories, Dreams, Reflections* (New York: Pantheon Books, 1963), p. 354.
4. C. G. Jung, *Letters*, vol. 2, Gerhard Adler, ed., Trans. R. F. C. Hull (Princeton: Princeton University Press, 1975). The extant letters of C. G. Jung have been collected in two volumes. The relevant references to how he happened to write *Answer to Job* are found in volume 2 on pages 17, 20, and 21. There are also many other references to *Answer to Job* scattered throughout this collection.
5. C. G. Jung, *Psychology and Religion: West and East* in *Collected Works*, vol. 11 (New York: Pantheon Books, 1963), p. 383, fn. to par. 600.
6. Jung, *Letters*, vol. 2, p. 120.
7. Jung, *Letters*, vol. 1, p. 338.
8. At this writing, May's book is not yet published.
9. My thanks to James R. Campbell of Chicago for this insight.
10. Jung, *Collected Works*, vol. 11, p. 383, fn. to par. 600.
11. For a more complete treatment of this problem, see my book *Evil: Shadow Side of Reality* (New York: Crossroad, 1981), chap. 9.

12. Marilyn Nagy, "Jung and Kaufman: The Father Complex" in *Psychological Perspectives*, Spring 1983, p. 114.
13. Edward Edinger, *The Creation of Consciousness* (Toronto: Inner City Books, 1984). Cf. his article "Depth Psychology as the New Dispensation: Reflections on Jung's Answer to Job," *Quadrant*, Winter 1979.

# 10 Reactions to *Answer to Job*

Among the people who reacted negatively to *Answer to Job* were two of Jung's closest colleagues. Eric Neumann, a Jewish Jungian analyst and one of Jung's closest friends, failed to see how Jung's idea that God was the author of evil was an improvement on the age-old answers religion has given to the question of the purpose for which creation exists and the origin of evil in human life. They sent arguments and counterarguments, albeit in a friendly spirit, in an exchange of letters.[1]

A not-so-friendly exchange of letters took place between Jung and Fr. Victor White. White was an early enthusiast of Jung's psychology; he was one of the first clergymen to see the importance of Jung's work for Christianity. White wrote several books presenting Jung's ideas to the public and showing their relevance for religion. For many years the two were the closest of friends and admirers. But White could not accept Jung's ideas on evil, and the two exchanged a series of letters in which the argument grew increasingly heated, especially when it touched on the doctrine of the *privatio boni*, so hated by Jung but espoused by White. Their friendship was all but ended when Fr. White became ill with cancer. Jung wrote him a conciliatory letter when he was near death.

Another theologian, this one a Protestant, who was an original advocate of Jung's psychology, was Hans Schaer. Like White, he too wrote publicly of his admiration for Jung's work, but when it came to *Answer to Job* Schaer objected to what he called Jung's sarcastic treatment of the subject. Jung defended himself in a letter in which he said that his sarcasm came from his hurt feelings. He notes in this letter that his feelings were wounded by God himself, though he also identifies himself as having to suffer because he was one against so many.[2]

In addition to these and other reactions by Jung's friends, there were also, of course, negative reactions by many people who had reason to be philosophically opposed to him. One of the most eloquent of these was the theologian H.L. Philp, who also wrote a book entitled *Jung and the Problem of Evil and* corresponded with Jung during its composition. If Jung had a feeling reaction against the doctrine of the *privatio boni*, seeing it as a pernicious idea, Philp had a feeling reaction against Jung's idea that God—or the Self—was inherently evil. The notion that, at the core of human personality and, by implication, at the core of the universe, there was an unconscious divine energy as intent on evil as it was on good offended Philp's feeling sensibilities deeply. He also felt that if Jung were right, the human situation was hopeless, for then "evil is inevitable and eternal and amorality is enthroned forever, for if goodness comes then evil cannot be far behind, and so the circle turns— for eternity."[3]

In the trial, Mapleson, though not espousing as such Christiansen's point of view, also rejected Savant's point of view. Of course, Mapleson's standpoint in the trial reflects my own. My critical reactions to Jung's ideas about evil and *Answer to Job* are both intellectual responses and feeling responses.

Intellectually I object to the book because there is no standpoint from which it can be criticized. If someone makes a statement that purports to contain a truth, it must be amenable to proper scrutiny and criticism. But there is no way *Answer to Job* can be constructively criticized, because there is no way to tell what kind of book it is.

For instance, is the book intended to be a scientific treatise, and are Jung's conclusions to be accepted as scientific hypotheses? One gets the feeling that we are to accept his conclusions as such, but the book does not provide the kind of empirical information on which scientific hypotheses are based. If the conclusions in *Answer to Job* are scientific statements, then we are, in fact, asked to accept them on some kind of faith, since scientific support for them is lacking.

Then perhaps the book is theology. We have already noted that Jung's conclusions do have the ring of theology—his denials to the contrary—but we are not allowed to critique the book from this point of view since Jung, in his introduction, explicitly denies that this is the case. A theological discussion of the matter is thus precluded from the outset.

Then perhaps the book is biblical exegesis. At first glance this is what it appears to be. Jung begins with the Book of Job and ends with the Book of Revelation, with references to other parts of the Bible scattered throughout. It looks superficially like a careful exegesis of the Bible in order to correct an erroneous view of the canonical image of God. As one Jungian scholar put it, referring to *Answer to Job*, "Jung turns to Genesis and proceeds now to offer a psychological interpretation of the whole biblical epic."[4] The problem is that Jung has not treated the whole biblical epic but only a few especially selected parts of it. We hear little or nothing of the patriarchs, the prophets, the psalms, or the teachings of Jesus found in the Gospels. The greatest omission, however, is the story of the Crucifixion and the Resurrection. The Resurrection, which is the centerpiece of the New Testament, receives only one passing reference. If *Answer to Job* is biblical exegesis, it is so one-sided and incomplete that it is bound to lead to a one-sided and incomplete conclusion. Jung also seems guilty of selecting certain passages and adopting certain disputed hermeneutic positions that support his argument. For instance, he is about the only modern scholar who believes the author of the Book of Revelation and the Epistles of John was the same person.

Then perhaps the book is a personal confession. Murray Stein argues that Jung wrote *Answer to Job* in a kind of countertransference to Christianity and that it was part of his attempt to cure Christianity of its ills. If Jung did cure Christianity of its ills, we would have to say that the operation was a success but the patient died. If Stein is right, the book is an unwitting, unconscious confession of where Jung was personally at the time. Confessional books can be valuable, but only if the reader is told of the inner experiences and processes out of which the confession emerges. Jung does not tell the reader this, so the value of the book as a confessional statement is limited. But even in this case the book would throw more light on Jung than on the subject he appears to be discussing.

But perhaps the greatest difficulty with *Answer to Job* is that in this book Jung made no distinction between natural evil and psychological or moral evil. It will be remembered that I made the point in the Introduction that distinctions such as this must be kept clearly in mind or we will fall into confusion in any discussion of the problem of evil. The difficulty is that the biblical Book of Job is about the problem of natural evil and why innocent human beings should be made to suffer. It is not a discussion of why human beings do evil things. But Jung has turned the book into a discussion of psychological evil. He uses the Book of Job to support his contention that God has an evil side that is responsible for the evils that come from the human heart. Job certainly experienced God's dark side in the form of natural sufferings, but he did not experience God as a power within himself prompting him to do evil. Job laments that God is treating him unjustly, but nowhere does he complain to God that he has made him a person who is necessarily bound to think, plan, and do evil. To the contrary, Job believes he is a good person who has led a good and faithful life. Because Jung failed to observe the distinction between natural evil and psychological or moral evil, he made a serious error when he used Job's story as evidence for his thesis that God portrays a Self within humanity that is evil as well as good. This might be the case, but the Book of Job cannot be cited as support for it.

As we have already noted, in the Old Testament God is frequently said to be the author of good as well as evil; it is not said that God prompts, desires, or underwrites the evil that human beings do. To be sure, as the prophet Isaiah had God say, God is the one who does good and who does evil. But when it comes to human beings, the Old Testament God expects justice to be done and mercy to be practiced. In the Book of Genesis,

God is so upset with the evil people do that he sends a flood to destroy most of the human race so he can get a fresh start. And in the prophetic books, God's prophets continually admonish people to do God's will, which is always to be faithful and just. Jung may be right that at the bottom of things there is a Deity who desires evil as much as he desires good, but there is virtually no support in the Bible for such a contention.

Moving from the intellectual to the feeling level, I find myself siding with Philp: if Jung is right, then life is a hopeless alteration of good and evil with no inherent purpose. For God, being composed of the unreconciled opposites of good and evil, will ceaselessly swing from one to the other. This would not be the case if God himself had a center in which the opposites were united. In that case God would be the equivalent of a whole composed of two sides. The wholeness of God, subsuming the opposites of good and evil, would then constitute a meaningful totality. God would then be the *Summum Bonum* that Jung so much decries. This would approximate the position of Eastern philosophy, except that Eastern philosophy says good and evil vanish in the Godhead and are meaningless terms.

But we have already seen that, according to Jung, God's opposites can only be united in human consciousness. God therefore has no center except insofar as a human being becomes conscious of his or her own good and evil sides. Just how this awareness of God's opposites creates a center in God himself is not clear. It sounds more like Freud's view that the best the ego can do is face the facts, see that we have within ourselves a life instinct and a death instinct, and try to make rational choices. If you have a devil in you it is always best to know it, but this does not necessarily change the devil.

To add to our pessimism, there is the unlikelihood that any but the most highly developed and conscientious persons could achieve the consciousness that appears to be necessary in order to reconcile God's opposites in the ego. Yet we are told that the unaided human ego is to do the task. This optimistic view of the ego is not borne out by our observations of the stubbornness, blindness, laziness, deceitfulness, and defensiveness of the human ego. The fact is, with only rare exceptions, the ego achieves consciousness only when it is forced to, and then only with the greatest difficulty. That it does so at all is because it receives a lot of help from a source beyond itself. From a religious point of view, God helps us in this monumental task; psychologically, we know that we can expect help from our dreams. But we could expect no help from Jung's God in this task since, though one side of God might want to help us achieve consciousness, the other side, by Jungian logic, is bound to defeat it. As mentioned, God is said to be composed of unreconciled opposites. If one part of the divine nature strives to help the ego achieve consciousness, the other side, which is intent on evil and destruction, will work against it. Under these conditions, how the unaided human ego could accomplish the Herculean task Jung sets before it boggles the imagination. There is thus the danger that Jung's position undercuts the ability to sustain the faith that is required if the difficulties of life are to be successfully endured.

## NOTES

1. Parts of Neumann's letter to Jung can be found in the German edition (but not the English) of *Memories, Dreams, Reflections*, pp. 376 ff. The whole letter from Neumann to Jung and Jung to Neumann can also be found in the German edition of *The Myth of Meaning*, by Aniela Jaffe, 1967, pp. 179 ff, but is not in the English translation. Cf. *Letters*, vol. 2, p. 493.
2. Jung, *Letters*, vol. 2, p. 28.
3. H. L. Philp, *Jung and the Problem of Evil* (New York: Robert M. McBride, 1959), p. 43.
4. Murray Stein, *Jung's Treatment of Christianity* (Chiron Publications, 1985), p. 166.

# 11 Faith, Hope, and Depth Psychology

Jung's position, discussed in the previous chapter, seems to share with depth psychology generally a certain hopelessness. We saw that when Freud looked into the unconscious he detected no sign of a divine power at work. Jung does see a divine power at work, but it is not a divine power from which one can expect the kind of help and saving grace that the human situation needs. This pessimistic conclusion is surprising since in so many ways Jung's psychology offers faith and hope to the soul. His idea of individuation makes it possible to feel that there is a meaning that runs throughout life, that no matter how bad or seemingly hopeless a situation, individuation is still possible. When Joseph was in Pharaoh's dungeon we are told that "Yahweh was with him." So Jung has told us that no matter what kind of dark dungeon life may have put us into God is with us—the Self working within us to bring about higher consciousness and inner growth. Certain superficial religions tell us what we want to hear—that by right thoughts or right prayer or right beliefs everything can be "all right"—but Jung dignified us by telling us that we could go *through* the darkness and find wholeness as we do so. Then suddenly we are told that the situation is hopeless after all. For, according to Jung, the Yahweh who was with Joseph is no help. He, and the inner reality he represents, is as evil and malicious as he is helpful and strengthening. For, as we have noted, if Jung's theory of the opposites is correct, God intends, in equal measure, our strengthening and sustenance and our senseless destruction. It is as though God has a moral bi-polar disease, swinging from one opposite to the other with no center of his own.

I have mentioned faith and hope. These are ancient religious words that one hardly ever hears in psychotherapy. Jung looked down on faith, which he regarded as the suppression of consciousness in order to blindly believe in things that cannot be known.[1] He takes up the ancient conflict between faith and knowledge and endorses knowledge versus faith because the latter is, for him, childish and based on dogma, not on any kind of experience. In fact, the soul requires both knowledge and faith if it is to survive in this world and find its proper goal in life.

True faith is not a belief in unprovable theological creeds or statements that is made possible by a childish abdication from the task of trying to understand. Faith is the motion of the soul toward God, or, if you like, toward individuation. It is not a matter of believing in something because it suits our wishes, but of putting one's trust and energy into something. In Greek, the verb translated in the New Testament as "believing" or "to have faith" (*pisteuo*) always requires the preposition "into" (*eis*) to complete its meaning. Faith must be put into something or someone that inspires and confirms it. Without a capacity for faith the soul loses its strength and gives up along the way.

In the early church after the third century there was a great tension between faith and knowledge (*pistis* and *gnosis*). But this was not the case at first. The teachings of Jesus in the Gospels aim at developing a new level of awareness in his disciples; his healing actions stem from and inspire faith. In the Fourth Gospel the way of knowing and the way of faith are both part of the same way. In the first, second, and third centuries many of the church fathers, such as Origen and Clement of Alexandria, termed themselves "Christian Gnostics," that is, "Christians-in-the-know," and developed hermeneutical methods that gave ample scope to *gnosis*. Only later, when faith degenerated into mere belief in creeds, and Gnosticism into a rival system of beliefs, did the conflict between faith and knowledge develop, leading to the unfortunate rejection by the church of the way of *gnosis* as over against the way of faith.

This is not the time to revive the ancient conflict, with its one-sided answers that force us to espouse the needs of one side of the soul against the other. It is the time to bring the two sources of the soul's power for living and growth together once more.

Yet the breach between faith and knowledge is with us again. Psychology espouses the way of knowledge. Jungian psychology, in particular, regards itself in many ways as the direct inheritor of the ancient tradition of *gnosis*. Christianity meanwhile clings to faith. But faith without knowledge is limited and, what is worse, fearful, for it tends to fear everything that it does not understand. Since it has rejected the way of *gnosis*, that includes a great deal. As a result, the faith of Christians today is in danger of being tragically truncated, and their fear of the unknown is becoming almost paranoid. Psychology, on the other hand, as we will see, cannot heal without faith. Nor is its knowledge sufficient when the soul is up against those crises in life that can be endured only with the stubborn strength that faith gives.

In fact, faith is the basis for success in psychotherapy. If a person were not moved by faith to see the analyst, he or she would never come. If during the process of psychotherapy the client loses faith in the analyst or in the process, it will not succeed. There is much talk in analytical circles of the phenomenon known as the transference, that peculiar and particular relationship that develops between analyst and analysand. There is much to be said about it, but at its heart is exactly this much-despised ingredient called faith. The fundamental ingredient in the transference is the client's faith in the analyst and the analytical process, no matter what other doubts may prevail in consciousness.

Faith in no way precludes knowledge. Knowledge and faith are a team. Both are necessary for healing and for individuation. Knowledge enables us to know ourselves, to understand the secret inner process that is taking place, and to grow in consciousness; it is noble and vital for healing and for individuation. But faith is vital too. It gives us the strength to go on knowing. It gives the soul the strength to go on living and trying and growing even when life becomes desperate. It gives us the capacity to keep on. Faith even leads to knowledge itself. It was, in fact, a strong conviction in the early Church that one needed to believe in order to understand. Certain things can be known only when we follow our faith and enter into certain experiences that only faith makes possible.

This matter of faith is of vital importance not only to the individual but to the health of society. So great is the need of the soul to have faith that if we do not find an appropriate place for this need we will put it in the wrong places. False leaders will arise and, if they have certain charismatic qualities, they will collect the unconnected need of the masses for faith. People will then put their trust in a variety of idols. The result can be seen in the catastrophic events of this century; a conspicuous example of this distortion is the faith the majority of the German people put in Adolf Hitler.

The question is not whether or not we need faith, but in what our faith will be placed. In psychotherapy, for a while the analyst may be a proper receptacle for our faith, but ultimately, if we are to grow into our own independence, there must be another place to put faith. After a certain amount of time in analysis, we begin to understand that we are not healing because of the analyst per se but from something within us. Then faith shifts, and we have faith in our own deep inner process. It is faith now in the Self, or God. But how can one have faith in Jung's God of good and evil?

If the soul needs faith, it also needs hope. One sustains the other. Faith gives us hope, and hope gives us faith. Hope also is vital to our individuation—indeed, to our very survival in life. If we lose hope we may die, if not literally, at least spiritually and psychologically. If faith needs to be put into something, hope needs to be grounded in something. But we must be careful of this hope that we find ourselves seeking. The ultimate ground of hope is not the hope that things will turn out all right, for they may not turn out all right. If we are confronted with an illness, a broken relationship, a failure in work or business, or the dangerous world situation, we may hope that it will "all work out." But what if it does not? Then our hope is destroyed.

James Stockdale, who survived eight years in Vietnam prisons, tells the story of one man who didn't make it. He said the man's problem was that he kept hoping. He believed every rumor that went through the prison: that the war would end, that Nixon would negotiate their release, that there would be an exchange of prisoners. As each hope proved groundless, the man gradually weakened, until he finally died of pure hopelessness. Others, like Stockdale, survived because they gave up this kind of hoping and concentrated instead on living for each other.²

Naturally, when we are up against a difficult situation we hope it will end. We hope we or our friends or family will recover from the illness, that the world situation will improve, that business will get better. But we must be prepared to fall back on a greater hope: that no matter how things work out there is a Reality behind it all in which hope can truly be grounded. But what is there to hope for from the God Jung envisions?

But maybe Jung is correct. It may be that there is no ground for hope and no place for faith. It may be true that the Self is equally good and evil and that there is no Reality beyond it that can be said to be a sustaining God who will be with us in the dungeon as Yahweh was with Joseph. Merely wanting there to be a God in whom one can have faith and hope does not mean it is so, and in the long run it would be nobler, as Freud urged, to face reality, whatever it is, than to live with an illusion.

But who can claim to know Ultimate Reality? We have had enough apodictic statements that begin with the words "God is this" or "God is that," especially when it is apparent that the absolutist statements of one person conflict with those of another. Even if one says "the *Self* is this" or "the *Self* is that" it does not sound much better. In theology and psychology it is time to practice the more humble attitude that physicists have learned to adopt. The most we can say is, "It appears that thus and so may be the case."[3] This attitude, in which a final judgment is reserved for such a time as the human race might possess more knowledge and insight than it does now, is expressed by Mapleson in the trial. Mapleson, it will be remembered, argued vociferously for his client Hyde, as a good attorney should, but when it was all over he confessed to Melanie Wood that he was not sure of many things. Nevertheless, putting aside Jung's more dogmatic statements, Jung did point out at least three facts that give the soul some basis for faith and hope.

*First:* There *is* an individuation process, and it does impart to a person something that seems to be inherently meaningful. Not only does the process of individuation help us get through life's difficulties, it can actually be hastened by them. It is not too much to say that without evil in the world and in human behavior individuation would not be possible, a point we will return to later. Another interesting aspect of individuation is that it seems to ignore death. At least as far as our dreams are concerned, they act as though life is a continuum and what we call death is only a transition.

*Second:* The life of our dreams is impressive. Dreams are as natural as nature itself, yet also deeply spiritual, because they seem to have in mind some future goal toward which the innermost personality is striving. They suggest that nature is not as natural as it looks, that the spiritual realm and the natural realm intersect. The natural and the spiritual may in fact be part of one seamless robe, a single reality that is divided artificially in the thinking of the ego.

*Third:* The dreams tell the truth. Whether they give us good news about ourselves and our life situation or bad news that we do not want to hear, they "tell it like it is." This makes them a reliable and helpful guide through life. As we will examine more closely later, this is not what one would expect if Jung was correct and the Self is partly evil.

Can we place hope in the Bible? Of course it depends on what meaning one extracts from the Bible. Jews extract one meaning, Christians another, and Jung still another. The Bible is also, of course, what can be called "secondary religious experiences." That is, it contains the religious experiences of other people, but not of ourselves. Nevertheless the Bible remains essentially a hopeful book and offers the soul a place in which to put faith. In the New Testament it does this by focusing on the one event that Jung avoided and disregarded: the story of the Resurrection of Christ. For here is a story that proclaims that no matter how bad, how evil, how hopeless things are, there is a positive Divine Reality that cannot be destroyed.

Many Jungians are afraid that people may try to turn Jungian psychology into a religion, that is, into a kind of metaphysical or dogmatic system with theological overtones. I share this apprehension. Jungian psychology is, when properly used and understood, exactly that: a study and knowledge of the psyche. When applied, it is a method of treating the ills of the soul. People can utilize Jungian psychology who haven't the slightest interest in dealing with the ultimate questions of life. A scientific study of the nature of the psyche and a pragmatic comprehension of how our knowledge of the psyche can be used in the treatment of psychological problems is one thing. The need to face and, if possible, to come up with some kind of answers to the ultimate questions of life is another. One is psychology and one is religion, and we need to keep the distinction in mind. Although I'm interested in the religious as well as the psychological side of human existence, I believe in maintaining this distinction. I think Jung, in certain places in his writings, confuses the two, if not intentionally at least inadvertently, with his choice of language. It is easy to do, since, as has been pointed out, though psychology is psychology and religion is religion, the one has direct, inevitable, and important consequences for the other. Jungian psychology, along with other psychologies, has implications for our religious or philosophical attitude that cannot be avoided. Nevertheless, we must keep the distinction as clearly in mind as possible, and for this reason I will henceforth in this commentary reserve the term Self for the psychological center of personality and God for the Ultimate Author of the universe.

The great problem of psychology, as well as religion, is where to locate the source of moral evil. Jung exonerated the ego from blame for evil, and placed it in the Self and, by implication, in God. However, could it be that the ego is not such an innocent character as Jung believed it to be? Could it be that having failed to see the evil in the ego Jung was bound to see it in the Self? It is to this that we now turn as we examine the relationship of ego, shadow, persona, and Self, as exemplified in the psychology of Fritz Kunkel. As we do, we will find ourselves dealing with the central issues raised by *The Strange Trial of Mr Hyde*.

**NOTES**

1. See *Aion* in *Collected Works*, vol. 9 (New York: Pantheon Books, 1959), paras. 269, 276, 277; vol. 11, paras. 285, 765; vol. 18, paras. 1511, 1635, 1648. However, as is usual with Jung, he occasionally refers to faith in a positive way, as in *The Integration of Personality* (London: Routledge and Kegan Paul, 1940), p. 289.
2. James Stockdale, "The Melting Experience," *National Review*, December 25, 1981.
3. Of course, if someone claims to have a divine revelation, the matter is settled for that person. I am speaking not as a theologian or metaphysician but as an observer of the psychological facts that are empirically discernible.

# 12 Why the Shadow Isn't the Devil

I have mentioned a number of people who were upset at Jung's *Answer to Job* and disagreed with his conclusions. I believe Fritz Kunkel was among them. This belief hinges on a distant memory. I began my analytical work with Kunkel when I was twenty-three years old. It was in 1953, and Jung's *Answer to Job* had recently been published. I met with Kunkel regularly for analysis and attended many of his seminars, but I was a very young man and he was much older and more experienced and I was not privy to his innermost thoughts. Nevertheless, there sticks in my mind the memory that when Kunkel read *Answer to Job* he was distressed and disappointed. For some reason this dim but persistent memory has stayed with me all these years. If I were in a court of law it would hardly stand up as evidence, but nevertheless there it is. Moreover, it is likely that Kunkel would not have liked Jung's position in *Answer to Job* because his own analysis of the relationship of the ego, shadow, and Self points in a different direction. What follows is Kunkel's material with some of my own added. As we will see, it deals with this matter of the origin of psychological evil.

So far in our discussion we have been concerned largely with the ego and the Self. But we have also noted in passing the existence of the shadow and the persona. Now it is time to look more closely at the shadow and the persona and the interrelationship among shadow, persona, ego, and Self. As we do, we will observe a subtle but important difference between Jung and Kunkel in the way they see these interrelationships.

In Jungian psychology we have the ego, which is roughly defined as the center of the conscious personality, and the Self, which is the much larger personality within us that embraces conscious and unconscious in a totality. According to Jung, the Self is the origin of our impulses and strivings to do evil. However, the ego is not as simple as it looks at first; in fact, the ego is, to a certain extent, unconscious even of itself. For closely connected to the ego are the persona and the shadow, psychological figures of which the ego is usually unaware.

*Persona* is a Latin word meaning mask. The *persona* was used by actors in ancient Greek and Roman drama, who wore these masks to represent the characters whom they were portraying. Jung took over the term and used it to refer to the face the ego turns to the outer world, to reality, to other people, and to collective expectations. The persona we adopt for ourselves frequently depicts the role we have assumed on the stage of life. The persona assumed by the clergyperson, for example, might project love and concern for others; that of the doctor might exude knowledge and authority, and so forth. The persona has come to imply something false, a mask that conceals one's real identity. At best it is a shallow representation of our true self; at worst it is a lie. In this way the persona has acquired a bad reputation, and "being oneself" is tantamount to shedding the persona and doing without it.

In contrast to the persona is the shadow. The shadow consists of all those qualities that could have become part of the structure of the ego but were repressed. These repressed qualities live on in the unconscious as an alter ego, a secondary personality. The shadow is close to the ego; in fact, it is a kind of ego in its own right. Wherever the ego goes, the shadow goes. In cases of split personality the shadow is even capable of taking over the personality entirely, as we know from studies such as *The Three Faces of Eve*. In such cases, when the shadow personality is in control it shows that it knows all about the ego, but when the ego is in control it is apparent that it is not aware of the shadow.

It is important to understand how Jung believes the shadow comes into being. The ego, in the course of its development, makes use of certain psychological functions and qualities that it finds useful and that serve its purposes. It identifies with these and integrates them into its structure. Of course, this is not done in a conscious way but as part of a life process. But in this process certain qualities that appeared as inferior, or did not meet the ego's goals or desires or the expectations of others, were denied. Repressed into the unconscious, they form the shadow. Jung wrote:

The shadow is the inferior part of the personality; sum of all personal and collective psychic elements which, because of their incompatibility with the chosen conscious attitude, are denied expression in life and therefore coalesce into a relatively autonomous "splinter personality" with contrary tendencies in the unconscious.[1]

The Jungian analyst Edward C. Whitmont puts it even more succinctly:

The term *shadow* refers to that part of the personality which has been repressed for the sake of the ego ideal.[2]

Note the terms *chosen conscious attitude* and *ego ideal*. The idea is that the ego has a certain notion of what it wants or ought to be. This is its ideal of itself. The position that the ego adopts in life is a matter of the culture in which it lives, its education, training, ideals, or psychologically one-sided development. On the whole, in spite of its one-sidedness, the ego is seen as a fairly innocent character.

On the other hand, the shadow is seen as demonic. To be sure, Jung once said the shadow was 90 percent pure gold, but the shadow is usually characterized in an extremely negative way. The shadow has been identified with primitiveness, violence, and cruelty. It constitutes the hidden powers of evil, lawlessness, and chaotic desires that, when released, bring about catastrophy. Out of the shadow comes inordinate desire for power. It is the inferior part of our personality where we are incapable, unadapted, irresponsible, psychopathic, and filled with infantile fantasies.[3] This picture of the shadow is reinforced by the way the figure appears (especially at first) in our dreams: a figure, the same sex as the dreamer, who is frightening, hostile, weak, malicious, deformed, and seemingly bent on destruction. And in fact, if the shadow personality is suddenly released, that is pretty much the way it acts.

There is a major difference between the way Jung saw the ego and the way Kunkel saw it. For Kunkel, the essential problem of the ego was its egocentricity, not its one-sidedness (though it certainly is one-sided), nor the fact that it has ideals that cause it to repress the shadow. Egocentricity is the term Kunkel used to refer to the single-minded, largely unconscious effort of the ego to defend and protect itself and to further its own ambitions. Neither the word nor the concept occur in Jung, with rare exceptions. However some contemporary Jungians do speak of "narcissism," about narcissistic people and a narcissistic ego structure. Kunkel's idea of egocentricity includes what is called narcissism today but with one important difference: Kunkel believed everyone was inevitably egocentric, whereas contemporary usage of the term narcissism in psychological literature reserves it for a certain few people who show obvious pathological symptoms. Kunkel also described the origin of egocentricity, its effects on personality development, and its many-faceted structure in far more detail than contemporary writers on narcissism. The idea of egocentricity, however, is not a new one. The Bible knows about egocentricity; whenever it speaks of people who are "hard-hearted" or "stiff-necked" it is speaking of people who are dominated bv their egocentricity.[4]

The Chinese book of wisdom, *The I Ching*, contains an interesting reference to egocentricity in Hexagram 59 entitled DISPERSION. The Image reads:

The wind drives over the water:
The image of DISPERSION.
Thus the kings of old sacrificed to the Lord
And built temples.

Sinologist Richard Wilhelm comments: "In the autumn and winter, water begins to freeze into ice. When the warm breezes of spring come, the rigidity is dissolved, and the elements that have been dispersed in ice floes are reunited. It is the same with the minds of the people. Through hardness and selfishness the heart grows rigid, and this rigidity leads to separation from all others. Egotism and cupidity isolate men. Therefore the hearts of men must be seized by a devout emotion. They must be shaken by a religious awe in face of eternity—stirred with an intuition of the One Creator of all living beings, and united through the strong feeling of fellowship experienced in the ritual of divine worship."[5]

In his books *In Search of Maturity* and *How Character Develops*, Kunkel elaborated on his complex theory of the origin and nature of egocentricity. These books, now out of print, have been conflated in a new volume of his writings entitled *Fritz Kunkel: Selected Writings*. For a full understanding of Kunkel's thought the reader is referred to this book. What follows is an extremely abbreviated summary of Kunkel's basic ideas.

Kunkel believed the child comes into the world with an innate trust and confidence in life and people. At birth the child is naturally whole.[6] This gives the child spontaneity, a healthy instinct to bond with people, which Kunkel called a "We"-feeling, and a lack of negative self-consciousness. The natural condition of the child is for the ego and the Self to be closely and naturally related. Out of this state of interrelatedness of ego and Self comes the capacity of the child to feel a close We-feeling with the significant adults in his or her life. Being at one with himself or herself the child is also at one with others. Sooner or later, however, this trustful We-feeling is broken by the destructive egocentric behavior that is consciously or unconsciously directed by adults toward the child. When this happens there is a separation of the ego from the Self as the nascent ego unconsciously creates a defense system to protect itself. It is clear that in his emphasis on the importance of children's early relationships, Kunkel thought along the same lines as Alice Miller.

This defense system is the basis for the egocentric formation of the adult personality. The rigidity of the egocentric adult personality, and the thickness of the shell that this egocentricity puts around the Real Self, depends on how early and how violently the original We is shattered by the egocentric behavior of significant adults toward the child.

The effects of egocentricity are profoundly destructive. Since egocentricity cuts a person off from the Real Self, the egocentric personality is uncreative and rigid, for creativity is the main quality of the Real Self. Since the posture of egocentricity is defensive the egocentric person does not live life fully, courageously, or completely. Egocentricity always gives the lie to life because it denies the expression of our true nature in its effort to protect the ego. Perhaps the most important fact is that insofar as we are egocentric we are incapable of loving others. In our egocentricity we can see other people only as allies to our egocentric goals or enemies to them. The capacity for love springs from the Real Self, from which our egocentricity has cut us off. Fortunately, most people live partly from their egocentricity and partly from the Real Self, which is why sometimes a person who usually behaves in a perfectly dreadful way every now and then comes through and surprises everyone with his or her creativeness and courage. In extreme cases, however, a person may be so encased in an egocentric shell as to be incapable of undertaking actions that show awareness of the feelings of others. Cut off from the Real Self, a person is also cut off from his or her humanity.

It will be remembered that earlier we spoke of Adolph Guggenbuhl's thesis that the psychopathic personality is born into the world incapable of eros and therefore commits crimes with no sense of guilt, regret, or human value. We also noted that one argument in favor of the idea that the Self is inherently evil, and that criminal behavior is archetypal, is that murders are sometimes committed coldly, without passion or reason, in a detached way that suggests there is no ego involvement. This may be so, but Kunkel's approach gives us another way of looking at it. Psychopaths may act as they do because they are so completely cut off from the Real Self, out of which their true humanity emerges. It is not that they are cut off from eros, but that is a consequence of their alienation from the Self. Moreover, their alienation from the Self may not be the original cause of their inability to modify their behavior by means of moral considerations, but the consequence of their choice to do evil. The coldly callous murderers who kill with no apparent moral compunctions may not be acting *without* ego involvement but with *only* ego involvement. They may have arrived at this psychological state through committing themselves to evil actions that so darkened and corrupted the soul that moral illumination and human feelings became impossible. This is the theme explored by Oscar Wilde in his novel *The Picture of Dorian Gray*. For if someone becomes completely egocentric, with no connection to the innermost Center from which our true humanity and human feelings emerge, this is the consequence.

Much the same thought is found in the spiritual philosophy of the American Indians. According to Indian psychology, the human being is a microcosm containing all the elements of the macrocosm of the universe. Everything in the universe has its representation in the human being, and all aspects of the life of the universe and the human being are to be related together in a unity. This totality within a human being was symbolized by the Indians as a cross within a circle, and at the center of the cross is the center of the human being. Joseph Epes Brown, commenting on this aspect of Indian psychology, says, "At the center of the circle, uniting within a point the four directions of the cross and all the other quaternaries of the Universe, is a human person. Without the awareness that they bear within themselves this sacred center, human beings are in fact less than human."[7]

It is important to note that we begin as innocent victims of evil and wind up as perpetrators of evil. That is, we begin as victims of the destructive egocentric influences of others but wind up, through our own egocentricity, passing these influences on to the next generation. Because egocentricity is an inevitable and tragic condition of human life, it can be regarded as a psychological version of original sin. When the Bible quotes the old adage, "The Fathers have eaten sour grapes and the teeth of the children are set on edge" (Ezra 18:2, KJV), it seems to have this "passing on" of egocentricity in mind. This may also be the psychology behind the statement in the Book of Exodus (34:7) that Yahweh "lets nothing go unchecked, punishing the father's fault in the sons and in the grandsons to the third and fourth generation." The central point for our present discussion is that in its egocentricity the ego has a great potential for doing evil.

There are as many ways of being egocentric as there are people in the world, and all we can do here is to sketch briefly the four most prevalent egocentric patterns, as named by Kunkel. One form of egocentricity leads people to refuse to stand on their own two feet. These people become inordinately dependent on others. They make a life profession of getting other people to take care of them and be their source of strength. They like people who can be persuaded to do this and hate people who refuse to do it. Their greatest fear is that they will not be able to get someone else to be their source of support. They are like vines that cling to a strong tree and would fall to the ground if the tree were removed, and Kunkel called them Clinging Vines.

A second egocentric pattern seeks admiration. Such a personality believes he or she needs and deserves praise; this person only feels well when on "center stage." People who offer the required admiration become "friends"; those who don't are enemies. The worst thing that could happen would be to become the object of derision, or to be second-best, or to be totally ignored. Such a person's life is dominated by the need for adulation and acknowledged success. Kunkel called them Stars.

A third egocentric pattern seeks security. This person wants to defend himself or herself by finding a safe place in which to hide. They are so vulnerable that they live by not exposing themselves to any of the hazards of life. Of course, in so doing they don't live life as it should be lived either. They may be selective in this. For instance, they might be aggressive or outgoing in certain circumstances, but when intimacy or emotion is required pull a shell over themselves that no one can get through. People who permit them to shun life they tolerate; those who might drag them out to face dangers, intimacy, or whatever is most frightening are feared and hated. Because such people withdraw into a protected place whenever danger threatens, Kunkel called them Turtles.

The fourth type of egocentricity leads people to seek power, specifically, to dominate others. Such a person is also afraid but seeks to overcome the fear by getting into a power position. "I'll get you first so you can't get me." These people *have* to be in control. If they have little power in actual life, they may content themselves with dominating their spouse or children. If they have the chance they become dictators. They too live in fear: of people who might overthrow their power. For this reason they can be extremely dangerous, as we know from the lives of dictators such as Stalin and Hitler who ruthlessly annihilated those they perceived as threats to their power. We can refer to such people as Tyrants or, after the infamous Roman emperor, Neros, the name Kunkel gave them.

Egocentricity is like a hard shell around the ego, shutting the ego in, shutting other people out, and preventing the energy of the Self from coming through. How hard this shell is depends, as we have seen, on how early in life and how violently the original "We" was broken and, as a consequence, how deeply separated the ego has become from the Self. The kind of egocentric pattern we develop will depend on whether we tend to have too soft an ego (Clinging Vine and Star) or too hard an ego (Turtle and Nero/Tyrant); whether our parents and other significant adults (including society) were overpermissive (leading to Clinging Vines and Stars) or too brutal and harsh (leading to Turtles and Neros).

People can also combine egocentric patterns. For instance, a tyrannical businessman who terrorizes his employees may be so fearful of intimacy that he shuns all emotionally significant relationships. People may also "flip" from one egocentric state to another. A Tyrant, when defeated, may become a Turtle, which is why bullies when beaten become craven. Similarly, a Star when humiliated may become a clinging and dependent person.

To the extent that we are egocentric we live in fear, under a sense of constant threat. We also live out and fulfill only a small portion of our personalities, because the egocentric life is a cramped life. It is like living inside a walled, heavily defended castle. Here we try to feel secure, but it does not occur to us that our castle is also our prison.

The egocentric ego may fool other people, but it cannot fool the unconscious. For example, the Star may win the admiration of some people who are taken in and do not know that this person is living a lie. Craven Clinging Vines may welcome the strong and tyrannical dictator, glad to lay responsibility for their lives at someone else's feet. Egocentric people make an alliance with other egocentric people for their own egocentric purposes. But the unconscious knows the truth: that it is all a sham and a lie. The Self knows that the true reasons for life are being ruthlessly denied, no matter how popular and apparently successful the egocentric pattern seems to be.

For this reason, life itself conspires against our egocentricity. To the extent we are egocentric we live under a constant pressure: from the Self, which will not be denied and which our egocentricity has turned into an enemy. Eventually our egocentric world always collapses. The longer we live, the harder we have to work to keep our egocentric patterns functioning, and the less effective they are. In the end, death itself is the ultimate threat to the egocentric ego.

It must be emphasized that it is not the ego per se that is at fault. The ego, when it is what it is meant to be, that is, the representative in life of the Self, is strong and glorious and creative. It is the egocentric ego that, because it is a distortion of what it ought to be, produces evil. It does produce evil, whether it is an evil noticed only by one's family, employees, or associates or an evil that goes down in the history books.

It is clear from all of this that, according to this view, the ego is not an innocent character at all. It is not just one-sided or too unconscious but is a positive instrument of evil. If this is so it is important to see it, for if the evil that lies in the egocentric ego is not seen for what it is, that evil will be projected into the Self. We are back to our question: Does evil originate in the ego or in the Self? Or is there some combination of these factors? We will return to this later, but first we must examine the nature of the persona and the shadow in the light of this concept of egocentricity.

As we have seen, the persona has a bad name. The Jungian analyst Thayer Greene, however, has defended the persona.[8] He claims that the persona is a perfectly legitimate organ of the psyche by means of which the ego projects the Self out into the world. Greene points out that the mask worn by the ancient actors was not used to *conceal* but to *reveal* to the audience the nature of the character in the drama. The persona, understood in this way, is the means that the ego uses to express the innermost reality of the personality in the external world. The egocentric ego, however, distorts the persona. Under the influence of the egocentric ego, the persona is not used to express the Self but to express the image of the personality that the ego wants people to see. For example, a clinging, dependent person will adopt the persona of a good, needy, and deserving individual in order to win support from people. A person who craves admiration may adopt the persona of an ingratiating person, or a jokester, or a saint in order to win the desired glory and approval. The persona, when distorted, thus becomes part of the lie that the egocentric ego is living, but when the persona is what it is meant to be, it is whole and sound.

Notice how often the expression "is what it is meant to be" is used. What we are dealing with here is a psychological version of the doctrine of the *privatio boni*. When everything in the psyche is what it is meant to be, it is sound and good. But when it is distorted, a "twist" enters the personality, and evil is the result.

We are now in a position to see the difference between Jung and Kunkel with regard to the origin of psychological evil, and also see certain misconceptions that Jung held with regard to the theory of the *privatio boni*. Consider the following quotation from Jung. It is taken from his *Visions Seminars*, and consequently is informal in style, but is all the more revealing of Jung's real attitudes:

To say the shadow is merely the absence of light is like the famous definition which optimistic people give of evil—that it is *nothing but* the absence of good, *only* a mistake. But when one sees how things develop in the world, one sees that the devil is really in them, that there is abysmal evil at work. One cannot explain the destructive tendency in the world as the *mere* absence of good or as a mistake made in something originally good. People say that at bottom man is good, but that is not true; one might as well say the opposite. . . .

And so our shadow really exists. It is as evil as we are positive and constructive in consciousness. . . . I mean the more desperately we try to be good and wonderful and perfect, the more the shadow develops a definite will to be black and evil and destructive. People cannot see that; they are always striving to be marvelous, then they discover terrible destructive things happening which they cannot understand. They may deny that such things have anything to do with them or, if they admit them, take them for natural afflictions, or try to minimize them and shift the responsibility somewhere else. The fact is that if one tries beyond one's capacity to be perfect, the shadow descends to hell and becomes the devil. For it is *just as sinful* from the standpoint of nature and of truth to be above oneself as to be below oneself.[9]

First, Jung is certainly correct that if one strives to be perfect in the common sense of the word, to be better than one is, to be wonderful, and so forth, it will create a split in the personality. Then the shadow will have to compensate an attempt to be one-sidedly good and perfect beyond what one's nature allows. There is no quarrel with this point of view. The issue is what is human nature at its core, and what is the source of evil? Kunkel's point of view, as we will see, is that the Self is creative. He does not identify it with "good" because everyone has his or her own idea of what "good" means. But he certainly disclaims that it is the source of the abysmal evil that Jung so correctly notes is at work in the world. Kunkel's point is that evil develops in human behavior when the ego tries to be what it is not. When the ego deviates from its true nature as derived from the Self, then there is a distortion and out of that distortion comes evil. He would quite agree with Jung's conclusion that it is "just as sinful" to be above oneself as to be below oneself, for any deviation from what is oneself is "sinful." Note that Jung does use the word "sinful." If we take this word in the New Testament sense—in which to sin means to miss the mark—if the ego deviates from its true nature in the Self it sins because it misses the mark. Oddly enough, in using such an expression, Jung indicates that in spite of himself he believes that evil arises from sin, which, psychologically defined, is the ego's insistence on opposing itself to the will of the Self.

But notice the words Jung uses in describing the theory of the *privatio boni*. He says those who espouse it say evil is "nothing but" the absence of good, "only" a mistake, a "mere absence" of good. These expressions—"nothing but, only a mistake, mere absence"—are not Kunkel's, nor do they come from any of those who espouse the doctrine of the *privatio boni*. They are Jung's expressions, and they show how he misread the doctrine. Evil is not a mere anything. It is evil. It is abysmal. It is destructive. Those who espouse the idea of the *privatio boni* agree with Jung that evil is just as bad as he says it is. The question at hand is how evil originated, and whether evil is fundamental to God's own nature. Or, in the case of the psychologist, whether evil is fundamental to the nature of the Self.

Now let us consider the shadow in relationship to the egocentric ego. Kunkel defined the shadow slightly, but significantly, differently than Jung and Whitmont. He wrote:

The shadow is a possibility of behavior and experience which completely contradicts or excludes the consciously acknowledged Ego pattern.[10]

As mentioned earlier, the shadow has qualities that are excluded from the ego because they conflict with the chosen egocentric patterns. For example, let us say that one's predominant egocentric pattern is to be clinging and dependent. In order to make that pattern work, certain qualities must be denied in oneself. Those would be the qualities that would impel toward independence and taking risks. One would have to deny all one's adventurous side in order to succeed as a Clinging Vine. These qualities of adventurousness, independence, and appropriate risk taking are positive qualities. This is why the shadow is indeed 90 percent pure gold. To be sure, when these qualities emerge from the unconscious where they have been repressed, they will look dangerous. Anything repressed emerges first in a distorted, bizarre, often violent form. But inside of this lies something positive and true to the nature of the Self.

If the predominant pattern is to be the center of admiration, what must be repressed would be our ordinariness. No Star wants to be ordinary, therefore we can't admit into consciousness our ordinary desires for love, affection, and the smaller pleasures of life, or our ordinary human failings, whatever those might be.

If our egocentric pattern is to hide from life's difficulties, what must be repressed is courage. How we will fear our own courage! It will live on in the form of the shadow. That figure will appear in our dreams as someone whom we hate and fear, but within the shadowy figure lies the gold of courage.

If the egocentric pattern is tyranny, that which must be repressed is vulnerability. If the injury is deep enough, all vulnerability will be repressed, and ordinary human decency may be completely obliterated. The true tyrant personality fears nothing more than loving another person enough so that this love can penetrate the shell, for that would dissolve the whole egocentric pattern on which that life is based.

This is why the shadow is always the adversary of the ego, as long as the latter is egocentric. It is also why facing and integrating the shadow has such a salutary effect on our psychological development. When this happens, not only do we add positive qualities to our conscious personality but our egocentric pattern is forced to change for the better. This is the clue to the inner meaning of the saying of Jesus, "Come to terms with your opponent in good time while you are still on the way to the court with him" (Matt. 5:25).

No matter how evil and destructive the shadow may seem to be, no matter how dark or feared a figure it might be in our dreams, no matter how inappropriately the shadow might erupt in waking life should it burst free of its chains, nevertheless the shadow embodies positive, not negative, aspects of the personality. Hence the shadow is not the ultimate source of evil after all, in spite of its disagreeableness to the ego. This is why Kunkel said the secret is that the ego is the devil. This is true in spite of the ego's pretensions to the contrary. For the ego is a great cheat, capable of perpetrating an enormous deception on itself and others. It is especially expert at using religious pretension and psychological jargon for its demonic purposes. For this reason the greatest evils are often done in the name of God. Kunkel wrote:

The ego without knowing it is always fighting on the side of evil and darkness, although it pretends to be a servant of light.[11]

Now it is time to look at the Self, particularly its relationship to the ego and the shadow. The Self is against the ego to the extent it is egocentric, but when the ego performs its proper function in life, the Self is the ego's greatest ally. That is why, in the quotation we noted earlier, the Book of Genesis tells us that when Joseph was in the dungeon God was with him. God is with the ego when it has been cured of its egocentricity, but against the ego when it is living a lie.

As for the shadow, it lies much closer to the Self than the egocentric ego does. No matter how outrageous the shadow might be, it is genuine, whereas the egocentric ego is not. The shadow has great energy precisely for this reason: in its genuineness it is in touch with the Self, the source of our psychic energy. The shocking fact is that in a showdown between the egocentric ego and the shadow the Self favors the shadow, even if it means the ego's eventual destruction. Kunkel wrote:

The startling fact is that the Real Self favors the Shadow in opposition to the Ego, in spite of the Shadow's destructiveness.[12]

We are now in a position to make some important distinctions between the shadow, the darkness in the Self, and the origin of psychological evil.

We really need two terms for the shadow. As we have said, the shadow in one sense is that in ourselves which could have been part of the ego but has been denied and repressed because it would have come into conflict with our egocentric pattern of functioning. Dangerous though this shadow may appear to be, it consists essentially of aspects of our personality that are vital for our wholeness. The other sense in which we can speak of the shadow is to refer to the dark side of the ego itself. We usually remain as unaware as possible of this, which means that we conceal from ourselves our true motives. The dark side of the ego is its egocentricity. This is far more devilish than the shadow. It is this egocentric aspect of the ego that is evil. Even when seemingly benign, it partakes of the nature of evil, because it gives the lie to life; and in exaggerated cases, as with a dangerous dictator, it may cause vast destruction.

We can now distinguish more clearly between the dark side of the Self and evil. When the egocentric ego encounters the dark side of the Self, it deems it a great evil. This dark side of the Self is akin to the "wrath of God" in the Bible; in fact, it can be said to be the destructive side of God as it operates within the human soul and in human life. The ego fears an encounter with the dark side of the Self just as Balaam feared the Malach Yahweh (dark angel of God) who crossed his path and threatened to destroy him if he persevered in his unholy intention to prophesy against the people of Israel (Num. 22). The prophets spoke of it as the "wrath of God" that will emerge on the Day of the Lord, and in a great day of tribulation will destroy all the unfaithful. It is the same aspect of God that the Epistle to the Hebrews refers to when it says it is a terrible thing to fall into the hands of the living God (Heb. 10:31). St. Paul also spoke of it when he said the faithless among the people of Israel, who in their wanderings through the desert enroute from Egypt engaged in sexual immorality and other sins, were demolished by "the Destroyer" (1 Cor. 10:10).[13]

This dark side of God may be mistaken for the devil, for when we unwittingly or wittingly oppose God, he appears in the form of an adversary. This was a point Kunkel often brought out: "God wants to train us for His creative purposes and we fail; our inner evil increases, and God's creative endeavor appears necessarily as 'organized evil'; God can be seen as the Devil. There is no other devil than God, misjudged and fought by Man."[14]

This is also why Nikos Kazantsakis had Jesus say in his novel *The Last Temptation of Christ*, "Someone came. Surely it was God, God . . . or was it the devil? Who can tell them apart? They exchange faces; God sometimes becomes all darkness, the devil all light, and the mind of man is left in a muddle."[15]

This dark and destructive aspect of the Self, however, is not intrinsically evil, because it destroys only that which is not fit to exist. Its ultimate purpose is creativity. However, it is the enemy to all egocentricity because our egocentricity is rigid and sterile and opposes the creative urges of the Self. Genuine evil, on the other hand, destroys that which is good and whole. The dark side of the Self destroys that which is *not* meant to be; evil destroys that which *is* meant to be. Darkness is as natural and positive an element in life as light, when viewed in this way. It is the Yin that balances the Yang. As said before, we must carefully distinguish between the words dark and evil or else any discussion of evil will fall into hopeless confusion.

We are now in a position to discuss the relationship of goodness to the Self. The paradox is that, if the Self is not evil (in the sense just defined), neither is it good, in the sense that people usually understand that word. As noted earlier, when we think of that which is good we may think of that which is law-abiding, obeys the rules, is perfect, has no blemishes, is entirely light with no spot of darkness, and so on. Such a form of "goodness" would lack wholeness and completeness and would be utterly sterile. If by good, however, we mean that which is whole or sound, the matter changes, for that which is whole will include the dark as well as the light, the Yin as well as the Yang. Paradoxically, that which is whole will contain imperfections. Its wholeness does not consist in its perfection but in its completion, which, as we have seen, is what Jesus had in mind when he admonished us, "Be ye therefore perfect, even as your Father which is in heaven is perfect" (Matt. 5:48, KJV). To put it another way, something is good when it is what it is meant to be. Then it functions correctly and in accordance with the will of God.

In fact, it is better not to use the term good at all when describing the Self but the word creative instead. We can hypothesize on the basis of what we know that the Self is ceaselessly creative. It is like a force that strives to bring about the most creative possible expression of life. It is because of its creativeness that it is also dark. If you are a writer and you compose a sentence, later you examine that sentence ruthlessly. You tear out this word or that, rearrange the meaning, reshape it until it is in the form that you want it. So with creative energy everywhere: it destroys that which does not serve the purposes of creation.

Now let us take a concrete example that will illustrate some of these things and then show how these points are brought out in *The Strange Trial of Mr Hyde.*

A good many years ago a woman in the parish church I had at the time made an appointment with me. She arrived with her slightly-built, listless, somewhat devious-looking junior high school–age son. The father was not there, and it was notable that he was never mentioned in the conversation that followed. The problem, the mother explained, was that her son needed home school instruction, but in order for the school to grant approval for such a plan persons of the proper authority had to sign appropriate documents recommending that this action be taken. Once the plan was approved, her son would be permitted to study at home under the supervision of a visiting teacher instead of attending classes at school.

The boy didn't appear to be physically ill, so I asked the woman why she felt this unusual arrangement was necessary. She explained that the problem was a gang of boys who were tormenting her son. They would insult him in the hallways, jostle him in the classroom, harass him in the boys' locker room, and generally make his life miserable. Indeed, the boy's life had become a hell, and since the school authorities seemed unable to correct the situation she wanted to remove him from this hateful environment.

The boy himself said little, but although he let his mother do the talking it was clear that he was in complete accord with her plan. The rough boys were described by the woman in the worst possible light and her son portrayed as an innocent victim who needed and deserved to be protected. In the course of our conversation she mentioned that the boy had seen a psychiatrist, of whom she spoke with great distaste. When I asked why she didn't like the psychiatrist, she complained that instead of signing the required document he just kept asking the boy the same question, "Why do you suppose they [the gang] are doing this?"

As soon as I heard this I knew they had seen a good psychiatrist who was zeroing in on the real problem: the boy himself. Apparently it was evident to the psychiatrist, as it was to me, that the boy was a first-rate sissy. A ready-made victim like this boy inevitably draws upon himself ready-made predators; this boy was a ripe candidate for the rough treatment he was receiving.

The mother and her son were not there for psychological counseling, and they rejected my attempts to help them gain insight into their situation even as they had rejected the efforts of the psychiatrist. It was clear enough, however, that the boy had an ego that was entirely too soft. He obviously had an over-protective mother who was ready to destroy what little masculinity the boy had, and the fact that the father was not mentioned suggested that he was either absent from the family or too weak to be effective. Thus the egocentricity of the father and mother was conspiring to produce an egocentric son. After trying unsuccessfully to help the woman and her son, I explained that I could not in good faith sign the document. They became angry and left; I had joined the psychiatrist on their blacklist. Since I countered their egocentric plans they hated me; if I had sided with them they would have sung my praises, but it would not have been love, only the response of the egocentric individual to an ally.

The egocentric posture of the boy was to be clinging and dependent, to seek protection and avoid risks. As long as he could create this environment he felt safe and secure; when he could not he felt anxious and threatened. The boy was so dedicated to his egocentric system of defense that he would remain in it as long as possible, even if it meant living the stultifying life of a stay-at-home. Somewhere in heaven, however, God saw this situation (I am speaking mythologically now) and sent the archangels down to do something about it. They stirred up the tough boys to make the boy's life miserable. For all their roughness one could say that the gang was God's agent in the matter, God's attempt to destroy the boy's egocentricity and reshape his ego into a fitting instrument for the creativity of his innermost Self. Putting the matter more scientifically and psychologically, the Self was against the boy's egocentric posture in life. The bullying boys were drawn to victimize him by the forces of the unconscious. The threat they constituted for the boy was aimed directly at his egocentricity: at the clinging, dependent, safety-seeking attitude he relied on to get along in life. They constituted a problem with which the boy, in his present state of consciousness, could not cope. It was therefore "be creative or perish." It was the dark side of the Self that was evident in the situation.

The boy had the persona of a "nice" boy. His pose was that of a good though needy person who deserved support and approval from other people more powerful than himself. He was a "nice" boy so others would approve of him, a quiet boy so others would not notice him or demand anything from him. All of this persona, however, was a false front. The persona had been distorted and forced to serve the egocentric ego, instead of performing its proper function as a means for the expression of the true personality in the outer world.

The boy's shadow had not made a direct appearance, but it is not hard to guess what it was like. In order to maintain his egocentric posture the boy had to repress and deny his capacity for aggression, righteous anger, and courage. These qualities would make up his shadow. If they appeared in a dream they might have been portrayed as a sinister, raging, dark, frightening man. If they had suddenly taken possession of him they would have come out in a potentially dangerous way. If the boy, for instance, had "flipped" and the shadow one day had taken over from the egocentric ego, and if a gun had been handy, he just might have shot and killed his tormentors. Of course the shadow would have received the blame. As we will see, "Mr. Hyde" always does.

The shadow, however, is exactly what the boy needed to free himself from the tyranny of the bullies and find his creative Self. In the course of our talk I made the outlandish suggestion that the next time the other boys pushed him around he might "sail into them," that is, fight back. Both the boy and his mother were aghast at this thought, and my stock with them declined rapidly. Had this happened, however, the shadow would have come up and brought with him the boy's masculine aggressiveness and courage. Of course he would have lost the fight and been left bleeding and crying with rage and frustration on the floor. Though physically hurt, however, he would have felt clean inside. Somehow he would have sensed something solid within him. Ego and shadow would have become friends. The loss of his egocentric posture, a thing he feared so greatly, would have been experienced as a great release. Even in his pain he would have rejoiced, and not even the principal's stern lecture against fighting in school could have taken from him a feeling about himself that he had never known before: self-respect. As for the bullies, their mission in life accomplished as far as the boy was concerned, they would almost certainly have left him alone after that.

Now we can look for the good and the evil in the situation. Superficially, this was a good boy and the other boys were bad. The good boy's shadow, had he been seen, would also certainly have been judged bad by the boy and his mother. But on a deeper level it was the boy's egocentric ego that was the bad reality, and his shadow, in spite of its potential for destruction, was on the side of creativity and authenticity. The boy's egocentric ego strove to please others and gain their support, but the Self was behind the shadow and against the ego. The boy's egocentricity made an enemy of the Self, which constellated its dark side. Dangerous though the shadow was, it was connected with the Center and the ego was not; consequently, the shadow had more energy than the ego, which was listless and lacking in vitality. The goals of the Self appeared to be to defeat and destroy an unproductive and sterile ego, and it was capable of resorting to dark measures in order to do so. The Self in such a case—or call it God's actions—would not in all likelihood have won the approval of the boy's Sunday School teachers. But drastic though the measures were that the unconscious powers were using, they were aimed at the renovation of a false persona and the destruction of a life-defeating, egocentric ego so that a healthy ego could emerge.

All of these points come out in Mapleson's argument in the trial. Mapleson defends Hyde by pointing out that Jekyll is the original source of evil in the situation. Jekyll's posture of being a good and dedicated person is nothing more than egocentricity. By means of this egocentric posture Jekyll presents a false front. He lives a lie and thus creates the fatal distortion in the personality that brings about the evil deeds of Hyde. What people mistake for Jekyll's goodness is only his persona, which has been distorted and brought into the service of the egocentric ego. Hyde too is a distorted figure, a caricature of what the qualities he embodies ought to be, but he is the creation of Jekyll's false ego. Hyde, Mapleson points out, intends Jekyll's destruction, and behind this lies the energy of the Self. That is why Mapleson can make the shocking statement that God favored Hyde over Jekyll.

The lack of a feminine influence is pointed out by Mapleson because the feminine principle would have permitted the various conflicting parts of Jekyll's personality to relate. The suppression of the feminine came about because the feminine did not fit into Jekyll's egocentric desires. Since Jekyll loved only himself, why did he need to love a woman? The result is that when feminine figures appear in the story they too are distorted. All the figures central to Jekyll and Hyde are distorted. They are evil or deformed because they are not what they ought to be. Of course this is reminiscent of the *privatio boni,;* which says that evil comes about when something falls away from what it ought to be. In fact, the story is a psychological version of that doctrine, a study in how the egocentric ego allows evil to exist through its betrayal of the good.

We have seen that the egocentricity of the ego can verge on the demonic. We have also seen that if we fail to see the evil in our ego's false posture in life we will certainly project it into the Self. We have noted that the egocentric ego, like the devil himself, according to the author of the Fourth Gospel, is a father of lies, and that if individuation is to take place we must have the harrowing and cleansing experience of seeing the truth about ourselves. We have noted that our egocentricity appears to originate from tragic early childhood experiences. For this reason it can be said that we start out as the innocent victims of evil, but wind up being its perpetrators. Neurosis is a manifestation of this egocentricity. The question still remains, however, whether all evil is originated by the egocentric ego.

Granted, as Kunkel once said, that the ego can be a devil, is it the source of all the devilry of this world? Or does evil also have an archetypal basis? It is to this question that we now turn.

## NOTES

1. C. G. Jung, *Memories, Dreams, Reflections* (New York: Pantheon Books, 1963). Glossary, p. 386.
2. Edward C. Whitmont, *The Symbolic Quest* (Princeton, N.J.: Princeton University Press, 1969), p. 160.
3. C. G. Jung, *Collected Works* (New York: Pantheon Books, 1964), Vol. 10, p. 218, "Fight with the Shadow."
4. Cf. Ezekiel 3:7, Exodus 32:9, Deuteronomy 9:6, or Acts 7:51, to mention just a few of the main references of this kind to be found in both the Old and New Testaments. The Reverend Ted Dobson has also called my attention to the "Enneagrams" of ancient Sufi thought, which bear a striking resemblance to Kunkel's idea of egocentricity.
5. Richard Wilhelm, tr., *The I Ching*, 2d ed. (New York: Pantheon Books, 1961), p. 243, first section.
6. Except that negative prenatal influences may affect the personality before birth.
7. Joseph Epes Brown, *The Spiritual Legacy of the American Indian* (New York: Crossroad, 1986), p. 36.
8. See his article "Confessions of an Extravert," *Quadrant*, Winter 1975.
9. C. G. Jung, *The Visions Seminars*, book one (Zurich: Spring Publications, 1976), p. 213. Italics mine.
10. John A. Sanford, *Fritz Kunkel: Selected Writings* (New York: Paulist Press, 1984), p. 164.
11. Ibid, p. 387.
12. Ibid, p. 389.
13. The Greek word is ὀλοθρευτής. In the Book of Revelation, Satan is also called the Destroyer, but another Greek word Ἀπόλλυων is used to speak of him (Rev. 9:11).
14. Fritz Kunkel, *Creation Continues*, first edition, p. 104, now out of print.
15. Nikos Kazantsakis, *The Last Temptation of Christ* (New York: Simon and Schuster, 1960), p. 15.

# 13  Evil as an Archetype

As we have seen, unless we are careful to state clearly what we mean by our terms, any discussion of evil will fall into confusion. For this reason a distinction was drawn in the preceding chapter between the dark side of the Self and intrinsic evil. We also distinguished between "goodness" as commonly conceived, and creativity. It is now necessary to go further into these distinctions.

It is harder to define what is meant by the good than what is meant by evil, for the word "good" evokes many diverse associations in our minds. For some people being good might mean obeying all the rules, being an obedient follower of that which is collectively sanctioned, even though such a life might become dull and unfulfilling. People who are good in this way will lose touch with their shadow and so will lack depth and vitality. For others, goodness might mean that which is perfect, has no blemishes, impurities, or darkness. Such an idea of goodness would leave out everything paradoxical, and the dark would not be there to complement the light. A God who is good, when goodness is thought of in these terms, would be imagined as a deity with no trace of darkness or paradox, a deity capable only of saccharine love. Such a deity would be a Sunday School god whose desires and commandments coincide in a marvelous way with the dictates of the established value systems of church and society, no matter how narrow, uncreative, and confining these might turn out to be.

None of these notions of goodness are what I have in mind when I speak of the goodness of God or the Self. As mentioned, Jung's attack on what he understood to be the canonical God-image in the Bible is a helpful corrective to any infantile images of God that may still be lingering in our minds, and for this I am grateful. But most people with any psychological experience or spiritual depth have long since left behind any such puerile notions of the goodness of God.

We could say that the good is that which is whole, that if something is whole it is sound and is as it ought to be, and that this is what makes it good. Evil then, as indicated earlier, would be the power that seeks to destroy wholeness. This is a strong definition of goodness, especially if we keep in mind that wholeness does not mean perfection in the sense of something without any blemish or imperfection.

However, since the word good means so many things to so many people, perhaps it is better not to use it at all when describing the nature of the Self. For this reason, as we have seen, a better description of the essence of the Self would be *creative*.[1] That which is creative, as was hinted earlier, seeks to bring about ever new and more creative forms of life and consciousness. Evil, then, would be whatever opposes the creative goals and energies of the Self. To say that the Self is creative also means that truth emanates from it, since one cannot build anything creative on a foundation of falsehood. Psychologically this means that if we are to develop in accordance with the Self we must see the truth about ourselves. It is also a way of saying that the Self, precisely because it is creative, has a fundamental integrity to it. This is the way Kunkel saw the Self. For Kunkel the Self was ceaselessly trying to create, and the process of individuation was a process of continuing creation. It was full of twists and turns, paradoxes and surprises precisely because the Self is creative and therefore unpredictable.

How about the Self as love? The New Testament describes God as love, and if the Self is the image of God in the psyche, is it not also love? I believe it probably is. However, as far as the Self is concerned, the first manifestation of the Self we are likely to experience is its dark side, as it destroys that within us that is not fit to exist. We may then learn to understand its creativity as we realize the creativity of unconscious processes and the creative nature of the individuation process. Behind this creativity lies love, but it is often (though not always) the last aspect of the Self to be realized. Jung himself describes his experience with the nature of God as love in the last chapter of his autobiography *Memories, Dreams, Reflections*. However he did not, as far as I know, integrate this experience into his understanding of God as the author of evil as well as good.

Jung's idea of the Self as the origin of psychological evil raises questions about its integrity. Evidence that Jung is wrong, however, comes from those expressions of the life of the Self—our dreams. As mentioned earlier, dreams show us our inner situation as it is. It was Jung himself who first brought this to the attention of the world, for the truthfulness of dreams was a vital point of disagreement between Jung and Freud. Freud believed that dreams have a manifest dream content and a latent dream content. The manifest dream content is the surface appearance of the dream that actually conceals its true, inner meaning. Jung argued that dreams conceal nothing; to the contrary they unabashedly reveal a point of view that the conscious personality often finds embarrassing. The reliability of dreams as a guide to our development is a cornerstone of Jungian therapy; virtually every Jungian therapist has an unshakeable faith in the power of the dream to help us come to consciousness. In this belief that dreams speak the truth, Jungian psychology agrees with dream theories of ancient people all over the world. The American Indians, for example, saw dreams as sent by the Great Spirit to guide our souls in this world; without the light they shed on our path the soul would wander in error and confusion.

The reliability of dreams as a guide is not what one would expect if the Self were evil as well as good. One aspect of evil, as the Fourth Gospel makes clear, is to deceive, and the devil is called the "father of lies."[2] We would have to suppose, therefore, that if the Self is evil as well as good the dreams would be as likely to deceive us as to guide us, but fortunately this is not the case. Jung's point of view in *Answer to Job* notwithstanding, he himself had this faith in dreams.

The dreams do not lie, but the ego lies when it is acting in its own interest as perceived through its egocentricity. In fact, one of the hallmarks of egocentricity is exactly this tendency to avoid the truth. The egocentric ego lives a lie and tells lies, both to itself and to others. It is so used to doing this that it may be entirely unaware of what it is up to and fancy that its lies are the truth. This is what gives the egocentric ego the capacity to become demonic. It is this tendency toward self-deception that Kunkel had in mind when he said the secret is that the ego is the devil.[3]

This appears to be the point that Scott Peck makes in his book *People of the Lie*.[4] Peck argues that the progenitors of evil are laziness and narcissism. He sees evil as a disease, a personality disorder that leads to the abdication of personal responsibility. When people refuse to see their own sins, evil arises.

Narcissism is a fashionable word in psychological discourse today that is roughly the equivalent of Kunkel's word egocentricity. The difference is that psychologists reserve the word narcissism for certain people who exhibit marked personality disorders. Even Peck seems to believe that this tendency to evil exists only in people who are ill. On the other hand, Kunkel recognizes that we are all prone to egocentric self-deception. Some people may be especially glaring examples of it, but none of us can claim to be free of this universal tendency. Egocentricity is a kind of psychological original sin from which we all need to be redeemed.

The antidote to this evil is psychological honesty, that is, the development of the capacity to be honest with oneself about oneself. This kind of honesty is the *sine qua non* of spiritual and psychological development. One reason that psychotherapy is such a long and laborious process is that the ego's self-deception must be overcome and replaced by an attitude of searching self-examination.

The extent and dangers of our egocentricity are far deeper than it is generally supposed. Being egocentric is not merely a matter of occasionally succumbing to envy, or sacrificing a bit of moral integrity in order to keep our job, or wanting a bit more praise than we deserve, or avoiding situations we should not avoid because they frighten us. For our egocentricity gives to our personalities a distortion that can be fatal to our moral integrity, our capacity to lead a meaningful life, and our ability to become whole. When the distortion is too great, then, as mentioned, the demonic enters the picture. Moreover, this distortion not only affects the ego but runs throughout our whole character, because when the ego is not what it ought to be, neither are the persona nor the shadow what they ought to be. As noted earlier, it is our egocentricity that creates and then represses the shadow and distorts the persona to its own service instead of allowing it to be a socially useful way in which the Self can be expressed.

As we have seen, Jung, in *Answer to Job*, argues that evil comes from the promptings of the Self, and the ego is a relatively innocent character who happens to be one-sided, out of balance, and out of proportion, but not the originator of evil. Yet Jung often talked of the origin of evil in a different way. Consider the following comments that Jung made when he was reflecting on the horrible things that people have done in the name of Jesus:

You see, the progress of man has caused such monstrosities to exist, because he only advanced on one side and the other was left in the dark undeveloped. So the intellect, for instance, was allowed to produce monstrosities, the most monstrous convictions or devices; and the feeling was allowed to develop monstrosities because it was not counterbalanced by the mind in antiquity; everything got out of proportion and that created the most hellish beings.[5]

There is no mention here of egocentricity because Jung lacked the concept, but in all other respects it is clear that in this passage Jung sees evil as originating from a malfunction in the ego. It is not what it ought to be, and out of this condition in the ego come "monstrosities" and "the most hellish beings," in short, evil. Now a monster is a distortion; if something does not turn out to be what it ought to be, it is a monster. Add to the notion of the unbalanced nature of the ego its egocentricity, and Jung's statement coincides with the point I have been trying to make. Jung concludes:

For nature can only be completely unconscious; with consciousness begins the deviation from the course of nature. Therefore we have such difficulty with our nature; we always deviate, and so we always have to try to find the way back. Our consciousness always tries to persuade us that we could go very far away. Our whole civilization has been a gigantic attempt to force nature into our rational schemes. The machine age was an attempt at a substitution, as if we could escape the unconsciousness of nature. Conscious rationalism went too far and had to return; it was a monstrosity that caused an extraordinary chaos. You see this bit of vision shows that it is not only the animal instinct which has been lost and suppressed, but also an insight into the real character of our conscious attempts to master nature; it really produces perversities.[6]

Here Jung speaks of the monstrosity produced by an ego with an exaggerated conscious rationalism that tried to get away from its true nature, and in so doing deviated from its true nature. Notice the word deviation, a hallmark term of the idea of the *privatio boni*, which says that evil comes when there is a deviation from the good. The result of all this, which adds up to egocentricity, is chaos and all manner of perversities. No talk here of the Self being the cause of such evils; the ego can do it on its own.

But now we come to another question: Does the egocentric ego create the whole world of evil, or does it simply ally itself with evil and so partake of the nature of evil? If we say that the egocentric ego allies itself with evil, we express our belief in an evil that lies beyond the ego but enters into and dominates the ego to the extent that it is egocentric. In Jungian parlance this is a way of saying that evil is not only a matter of personal ego psychology, but it has an archetypal basis. An act of moral evil would then be a compendium of the egocentric ego and archetypal evil. The figure of Satan would then personify not only the ego's lying tendencies but also the evil that lies in the archetypal realm.

It would appear that there is a realm of archetypal evil. This archetypal evil is not a core aspect of the Self but is part of the archetype of choice, a possibility that is necessary if choice is to exist. And choice is fundamental to the individuation process, or, to put it theologically, to the knowledge of God.

Psychological and spiritual development involves the making of choices, as does life itself. Whether they are made consciously or unconsciously makes no difference as far as their psychological and spiritual consequences are concerned. Our capacity—and necessity—for choice making is perhaps the most important quality distinguishing us from other forms of animal life.

Life, and the Self, hold us responsible for our choices no matter how we arrive at them. The fact that we may be unconscious of the choices we are making does not shelter us from their consequences. There is a certain impartial ruthlessness in the spiritual life just as there is in nature. If you hike into the wilderness without taking proper precautions and are caught in an unexpected snowstorm you may very well freeze to death. In our spiritual and psychological lives the consequences of our choices are equally impartial and ruthless. Even though two Jungian analysts wrote a book called *Man the Choice-Maker*,[7] Jungian psychologists generally, along with other psychologists, pay little attention to the matter of choice. This is understandable when it comes to psychologists such as the behaviorists, for they don't believe there is such a thing as choice: human behavior is just a matter of conditioning. But Jungian psychology believes in the archetypes, and there surely must be an archetype for something as fundamental to human existence as choice.

Evil, and its personification in the figure of Satan, is part of this archetype, for if evil did not exist neither would choice. The archetype of choice requires that there are alternatives from which to choose. A decision to say yes to something must carry with it the possibility of saying no. A choice toward the good must also have a choice toward the bad. When a moral or spiritual choice is to be made there must be alternatives: One either chooses for or against the purposes of the Self or God. If there were not such choice in the world, spiritual development and psychological consciousness could not take place, and individuation would be impossible.

However, this does not place evil at the heart of the Self. Like all archetypes, the archetype of choice, which includes evil, is subordinate to the Self. To put it theologically, we could say that evil is allowed by God's plan but does not express God's intent.[8]

A clear example of evil as part of the archetype of choice is found in the story of the temptations in the wilderness found in the fourth chapter of the Gospel of Matthew. In this story Jesus has just received the Holy Spirit and is empowered by God to do a divine work. Immediately after this he goes into the wilderness and there encounters Satan, who tempts him with three choices. It is not hard to see that all three temptations involve using his divinely given power for egocentric purposes. The first temptation is to turn bread into stones; if Jesus had done this he would have been a great Star, the most admired man of his time, if not of all history. The second temptation was to cast himself off a cliff and be saved by the angels; this too is a temptation to star, to become the object of wonder and admiration. The final temptation is to become the ruler of all the kingdoms of the world, a clear temptation to tyranny and power. We could hardly ask for a clearer representation of evil as the archetype of choice. Nor could we ask for a clearer representation of the way that the tendency of the ego toward egocentricity can allow evil to operate and make the ego an ally of evil rather than of God. The psychological ground of evil lies in choice, will, and deed; it is the archetype that stands behind all of these typical manifestations of the life of the psyche.

This way of looking at the role of evil in psychological development also says something about what we can expect from the world. We must, of course, do all we can to make the world a livable place, correct its injustices, and curb the power of evil, but we cannot expect the world to be a perfect place. As a friend of mine once reminded me, the world isn't supposed to work; it is only supposed to be a realm in which individual consciousness can develop.[9] Trying to rid the world of evil is like trying to keep weeds out of the lawn and garden; we have to work at it all the time. We know that if after great diligence we have pulled up virtually every weed, plentiful seeds hidden in the ground will soon thrust up others. Good gardeners therefore accept it as part of their work to continually try to rid their garden of weeds, for if they did not, the weeds would take over. So it is with evil in the world. We must work to rid the world of evil, beginning with ourselves, but we must also know that our task will never be complete, for the seeds of evil are embedded in the archetypal structure of the psyche. Evil is always ready to spring up again, and for this reason we can never be too sanguine about the world. On the other hand, neither should we be too discouraged. For this is evidently the way the world is meant to be. This is what makes the world an arena in which individuation can take place.

## NOTES

1. As so often happens, Jung is contradictory. When he is speaking "off-the-cuff," he describes the nature of the Self as creativity. Such a description of the Self contradicts his description of the Self as the author of psychological evil. These contradictory statements by Jung, which he himself apparently did not notice, create difficulties for students of his psychology. An example of Jung's perception that the Self is creative is the following, taken from his *Visions Seminars*, book I, pp. 134–35:

   You see, it is tremendously important that people should be able to accept themselves. Otherwise the will of God cannot be lived: they are somehow cramped or blighted; they don't really produce themselves so as to express the whole of the creative will which is in them; they assume a better judgment than God himself, assume that man ought to be so and so. In that way they exclude many of their real qualities. . . . It is only our minds that cause such feelings and make that tremendous and blasphemous assumption that we know better than the will within us.

2. See John 8:44, cf. Acts 5:3.
3. In this connection it is interesting to note the meaning of the word Antichrist which has been made so much of in Christian thought. In the New Testament the word occurs in the First and Second Epistles of John. The

Greek word is *antichristos* (αντιχριστος). It is a compound of the preposition *anti* (αντι) and the noun Christ (χριστος). In Greek, as in other Indo-European languages, prepositions are often combined with verbs, and occasionally nouns, in order to form a new word with a more complete emphasis. The preposition *anti* is often translated "against," but sometimes the intended meaning is "substituted" or "in place of." This is the case, for instance, in Matthew 2:22: "But when he learnt that Archelaus had succeeded his father Herod as ruler of Judaea he was afraid to go there." The literal translation would be: "And having heard that Archelaus was king of Judaea instead of his father Herod." The Greek translated "instead of" is *antì toû patrós,* a clear illustration of the use of *anti* to mean "instead of," or "in place of." It has been suggested that the complete meaning of Antichrist would be "one who has assumed the guise of Christ in order to deceive his people" (p. 105 of *Lexical Aids for Students of New Testament Greek,* by Bruce M. Metzger, published by the author, 1962). What then if the word Antichrist refers to one who is against Christ because he has placed his ego in a position of power instead of Christ? Psychologically speaking, if we take Christ to be the true or whole personality, it is the egocentric ego that is set up instead of him. Kunkel no doubt had this setting up of the ego in place of the true Self in mind when he spoke of the ego as the devil.

4. M. Scott Peck, *People of the Lie: The Hope for Healing Human Evil* (New York: Simon & Schuster, 1983).
5. C. G. Jung, *The Vision Seminars,* bk. 2 (Zurich: Spring Publications, 1976), p. 423.
6. Ibid. p. 424.
7. Elizabeth Boyden Howes and Sheila Moon, *Man the Choice-Maker* (Philadelphia: Westminster Press, 1973).
8. To use an inadequate but perhaps useful analogy: when a child comes of age a wise parent ceases to try and direct that child's life and leaves the child free to make his or her own choices. These choices might prove good or bad, fortunate or unfortunate, but the parent knows that until the child is free to choose on his or her own the child will not mature. Thus the parent *allows* the child to choose, knowing the choice might be wrong, but does not *intend* that the child choose the evil over the good.
9. Thanks to Robert Johnson of San Diego.

# 14 Facing Uncertainty with Faith

I have argued that the points of view of behaviorism, Freudian-
ism, and most other psychologies have negative implications
for a meaningful worldview. I have also argued that Jung,
though allowing for the existence of a divine dimension at
work in the psyche, weakens the basis for any faith or hope
that there is a meaningful and trustworthy ultimate basis for
existence because the Divine, as he sees it, is as malevolent as it
is positive in its intentions. I have also argued that faith is essential in the healing process, for without faith the soul de-
spairs and gives up the struggle of life. It may be, of course,
that reality offers us no basis for faith. On the other hand, it is
not necessary to reach this gloomy conclusion, because the psyche itself gives us some basis for faith and hope. The fact that
there is that movement toward completion in life that we call
individuation, is something hopeful that can help us live life
with faith. If it is true that the Self is not evil, but creative, then
there is even more basis for faith, because in that case evil,
though real, is not at the heart of things.

To put it another way, only the Self, or God, can exist on its
own. Evil exists only insofar as it is allowed to by a Higher
Power. Furthermore, since evil is by definition a principle of
destruction, it cannot exist on its own, but only by virtue of
something more or less whole and sound that it can destroy. To
use an imperfect but perhaps helpful analogy, evil is like a disease. A disease exists only as long as there is a body that is more
or less healthy. When the health of the body is totally destroyed, death comes, and when the body dies the disease that
killed it ceases to exist. Thus disease always destroys that
which is the basis of its existence.

It is interesting to note that this is very much like the position toward evil taken by the ancient Chinese book of wisdom *The I Ching*. For those unfamiliar with *The I Ching*, a word of explanation may be helpful. *The I Ching* is founded on the ancient Chinese philosophy that if a person acts in accordance with the will of God (the Way of Heaven or Tao), then he or she will act properly. In every life situation there is a correct attitude that enables a person to do this. By means of sixty-four images, called hexagrams, *The I Ching* offers a way of meditating on which attitude and understanding is correct for life's many changing situations. In the edition of *The I Ching* by the sinologist Richard Wilhelm, a close friend of Jung, a commentary by Wilhelm accompanies the images or hexagrams. Certain hexagrams with their accompanying commentaries concern themselves with the nature of evil. Even a reader who is unfamiliar with *The I Ching* will be able to understand the import of what Wilhelm has to say about evil based on the meaning of these hexagrams.

For example, consider the reading for the sixth line of hexagram 36, and the commentary on it by Wilhelm. Hexagram 36 concerns a situation in which the sun has sunk below the horizon, representing a situation in which the power of evil is in the ascendancy. The sixth line reads:

> Not light but darkness.
> First he climbed up to heaven,
> Then he plunged into the depths of the earth.

The commentary reads:

Here the climax of the darkening is reached. The dark power at first held so high a place that it could wound all who were on the side of good and of the light. But in the end it perishes of its own darkness, *for evil must itself fall at the very moment when it has wholly overcome the good, and thus consumed the energy to which it owed its duration.* (Italics mine)[1]

Another hexagram that deals with the problem of evil is hexagram 23. This hexagram describes an evil situation that is developing; the dark lines in the hexagram are mounting upward to overthrow the last light line. This signifies that there is a disintegrating influence at work. As will be noted, Wilhelm sees the nature of evil, as revealed in this hexagram, as negation. Negation is the opposite of creativity. The thought is that evil cannot stand on its own because it cannot create; it can only destroy that which is created. The hexagram reads:

> The mountain rests on the earth:
> The image of SPLITTING APART.
> Thus those above can ensure their position
> Only by giving generously to those below.[2]

The reading for the ninth line—at the top—reads:

> There is a large fruit still uneaten.
> The superior man received a carriage.
> The house of the inferior man is split apart.

Wilhelm comments:

Here the splitting apart reaches its end. When misfortune has spent itself, better times return. The seed of the good remains, and it is just when the fruit falls to the ground that good sprouts anew from its seed. The superior man again attains influence and effectiveness. He is supported by public opinion as if in a carriage. But the inferior man's wickedness is visited upon himself. His house is split apart. A law of nature is at work here. *Evil is not destructive to the good alone, but inevitably destroys itself as well. For evil, which lives solely by negation, cannot continue to exist on its own strength alone.*[3] (Italics mine)

The viewpoint of *The I Ching* recognizes the paradoxical nature of evil without succumbing to a fatalistic attitude that evil is at the heart of the universe. It does not answer all the questions that we have about the nature of evil or even about the necessity of evil; neither have I answered all these questions, nor did I intend to do so. The truth is that we need to be suspicious of any psychological, theological, or philosophical position that *does* purport to answer all of our questions about evil. Any analysis of evil that has all the answers is bound to be wrong, for we are simply not in a position in our present state of spiritual and psychological knowledge to have these answers. If we assert too much—if we make too many categorical statements such as "God is this" or "God is that" we are certain to miss the truth.

It was Jung who once pointed out that anyone who claims to be in possession of the truth is going to miss the truth because he or she will cease looking for it. In the nineteenth century, physicists thought they had the answers to virtually all the problems of nature. But in the beginning of the twentieth century Einstein developed his theory of relativity, the atomic nature of matter was demonstrated, and quantum mechanics destroyed existing notions of causality. The world of the nineteenth-century physicist lay in ruins. So with us. Our spiritual and psychological knowledge has not reached a point where we can claim to have all the answers. In a century still to come people may find themselves thinking about life in a totally new way that shatters any premature, apodictic conclusions we may have asserted today as "final" psychological or spiritual truths.

This is why at the end of the trial Mapleson confessed to Melanie Wood that, though he had argued his best in defense of Hyde, he himself could not be sure about the matters that had been discussed. The strength of the position taken toward evil by *The I Ching*, and by the Gospels, is that they don't give us neat, tidy answers to our questions. It takes, of course, a certain amount of courage to live with such existential uncertainty. But perhaps it is necessary to live with uncertainty in order to develop the strength of the soul. It is easy to believe if one supposes one has all the answers, even though it actually amounts to living with an illusion. It is harder to live knowing that we don't have all the answers—as long as the door is left open for the soul to exercise the faith and hope it needs in order to make its way through the perils of this earthly existence.

## NOTES

1. Richard Wilhelm, tr., *The I Ching*, 2nd ed. (New York: Pantheon Books, 1961), pp. 152–53, first section.
2. Ibid., p. 100
3. Ibid., pp. 102–3.

# Synopsis of *The Strange Case of Dr Jekyll and Mr Hyde*

The story begins with a lawyer, Mr. Utterson, stumbling into the mystery of the strange door. Mr. Utterson, described as "lean, long, dusty, dreary, and yet somehow lovable," is taking his once-a-week walk with his friend, Mr. Richard Enfield, "well-known man about town." On this particular occasion, their way took them to a "by-street in a busy quarter of London." Here there was a mysterious door, with no bell or knocker, "blistered and distained," carved up by schoolboys and in general disrepair, yet no one had appeared for a generation to repair these ravages. "Did you ever remark that door?" Enfield asks the unassuming Mr. Utterson, and then proceeds to tell a strange tale. Enfield was coming home late one night when all at once he saw a young, powerfully built little man stumping along at a great rate and, coming the other direction, a little girl running hard down the cross street. The two met, but the man knocked the girl over and calmly proceeded to trample over her body, leaving her screaming on the ground. "It was hellish to see," Enfield related, "It wasn't like a man; it was like some damned Juggernaut." The girl had cried out, and her screams brought people running, including Enfield, who ran after the culprit and brought him back to the awful scene. The girl proved to be unhurt, but there was something about the little man that aroused the fury of the onlookers. Enfield saw a doctor who had been summoned "turn sick and white with the desire to kill him." And the women were "wild as harpies." "I never saw a circle of such hateful faces," Enfield related, "and there was the man in the middle with a kind of black, sneering coolness . . . carrying it off, sir, really like Satan." Since killing the man is out of the question, the crowd demands reparations from him for the sake of the child's family, and the ugly man finally agrees to pay 100 pounds. He then produces a key, goes through the strange door, and soon emerges with a check, which proved to be genuine, for the required amount of money. The check was signed by a well-known man in the town, a man, Enfield related, who "is the very pink of the proprieties . . . one of your fellows who do what they call good." Enfield supposed it to be a case of blackmail, that the ugly man had something on the good man, from the latter's youth perhaps, and out of respect for the good man's name in town, Enfield refrained from asking more questions.

Utterson is left deep in thought. "There's one point I want to ask," he says, ". . . the name of that man who walked over the child."

"It was a man of the name of Hyde," Enfield replies. "He is not easy to describe. There is something wrong with his appearance; something displeasing, something downright detestable. I never saw a man I so disliked, and yet I scarce know why. He must be deformed somewhere; he gives a strong feeling of deformity, although I couldn't specify the point."

Mr. Utterson is shocked, for he knows the name already of the man who signed the cheque! As we will soon see, the man is Utterson's client, the respected Dr. Henry Jekyll. The two friends make an agreement never to refer to the matter again, and Utterson thoughtfully returns home, goes to his safe, and pulls out Dr. Henry Jekyll's will. This strange document, drawn up only by the doctor, for Utterson refused to have anything to do with it, orders that in the event of his disappearance for three months, all of Jekyll's goods are to be bestowed without question upon Hyde. The will had been detestable to Utterson before, but now that he knows Hyde to be such a sinister and despicable character it seems to him worse and more inexplicable than ever.

In his agitation Utterson goes to the house of Dr. Lanyon, a mutual friend of Dr. Jekyll and himself, where he inquires if

Dr. Lanyon knows of the mysterious Hyde. But all that Utterson learns from Lanyon is that the two doctors, who once were close friends, have now drawn apart. "It is more than ten years since Henry Jekyll became too fanciful for me," Lanyon tells Utterson. "He began to go wrong, wrong in my mind . . . I see and I have seen devilish little of the man. Such unscientific balderdash," Lanyon exclaims, his face "flushing suddenly purple."

Utterson returns home but can no longer sleep. In his tortured mind he keeps seeing the apparition of Mr. Hyde, but, of course, he has never seen his face. If he could only see Hyde, Utterson thinks to himself, then perhaps the mystery would lighten and he could sleep once more. So Utterson begins to frequent the area around the mysterious door that leads into Jekyll's laboratory and, at last, his efforts are rewarded as he sees a young, deformed-looking little man approach the door and brandish a key.

Mr. Utterson stepped out and touched him on the shoulder as he passed. "Mr. Hyde, I think?"

Mr. Hyde shrank back with a hissing intake of the breath. But his fear was only momentary; and though he did not look the lawyer in the face, he answered coolly enough; "That is my name. What do you want?"

"I see you are going in," returned the lawyer. "I am an old friend of Dr. Jekyll's—Mr. Utterson of Gaunt Street—you must have heard my name; and meeting you so conveniently, I thought you might admit me."

"You will not find Dr. Jekyll; he is from home," replied Mr. Hyde, blowing in the key. And then suddenly, but still without looking up, "How did you know me?" he asked.

"On your side," said Mr. Utterson, "will you do me a favour?"

"With pleasure," replied the other, "What shall it be?"

"Will you let me see your face?" asked the lawyer.

Mr. Hyde appeared to hesitate, and then, as if upon some sudden reflection, fronted about with an air of defiance; and the pair stared at each other pretty fixedly for a few seconds. "Now I shall know you again," said Mr. Utterson, "it may be useful."

"Yes," returned Mr. Hyde, "it is as well we have met; and *à propos*, you should have my address." And he gave a number of a street in Soho.

"Good God!" thought Mr. Utterson, "can he, too, have been thinking of the will?" But he kept his feelings to himself and only grunted in acknowledgement of the address.

"And now," said the other, "how did you know me?"

"By description," was the reply.

"Whose description?"

"We have common friends," said Mr. Utterson.

"Common friends?" echoed Mr. Hyde, a little hoarsely. "Who are they?"

"Jekyll, for instance," said the lawyer.

"He never told you," cried Mr. Hyde, with a flush of anger. "I did not think you would have lied."

"Come," said Mr. Utterson, "that is not fitting language."

The other snarled aloud with a savage laugh; and the next moment, with extraordinary quickness, he had unlocked the door and disappeared into the house.

Mr. Utterson has seen Hyde, but his mind is no more at ease than before, for ugly though Hyde was, nothing "could explain the hitherto unknown disgust, loathing, and fear with which Mr. Utterson regarded him. 'O my poor old Harry Jekyll,' Utterson says to himself, 'if ever I read Satan's signature upon a face, it is on that of your new friend.' "

So Utterson decides to go and visit Henry Jekyll. He is recognized and allowed in by the butler, Poole, but Dr. Jekyll is out. Utterson thinks this especially strange since he knows Hyde to have entered by the side door, but Poole tells him that though the servants practically never see Hyde, they have instructions to obey him, and that Hyde often leaves and enters through the laboratory door.

Utterson is hardly reassured by this knowledge. As he trudges home he thinks that Jekyll must be in great trouble. Surely, he supposes, the ugly Mr. Hyde is able for some reason to blackmail Jekyll. Moreover, what if Hyde learns of the will which leaves everything to him? Mischief must be the result of that! Utterson decides he must help his friend Henry Jekyll. " 'If Jekyll will but let me, if Jekyll will only let me.' "

Two weeks later Utterson is invited to a dinner party and finally has the opportunity to talk with Jekyll. So for the first time in the tale we meet with the central figure of Henry Jekyll, who is described as a "large, well made, smooth-faced man of fifty, with something of a slyish cast perhaps, but every mark of capacity and kindness—you could see by his looks that he cherished for Mr. Utterson a sincere and warm affection."

Utterson manages to remain until after the other guests have departed and at last is able to talk with his friend and client about the matter of his will, and of the mysterious Mr. Hyde. But he receives little satisfaction. Regarding the will, Jekyll does not want to discuss the matter, but when Hyde's name is brought up, and Utterson tells how he has met the man, "The large handsome face of Dr. Jekyll grew pale to the very lips, and there came a blackness about his eyes. 'I do not care to hear more,' said he. 'This is a matter I thought we had agreed to drop.' "

Utterson persists, and Jekyll declares that his relationship with Hyde is indeed painful, and his position is strange, but that it is a matter that "cannot be mended by talking." When Utterson urges Jekyll to trust him, Jekyll says he is appreciative, but he can only tell Utterson one thing: "the moment I choose, I can be rid of Mr. Hyde." The conversation concludes with Jekyll asking for and receiving a pledge from his friend, Utterson, to help Hyde when and if Jekyll should no longer be here, for, Jekyll declares, "I do sincerely take a great, a very great interest in that young man."

But Utterson does learn one thing: that Jekyll and Dr. Lanyon have had a more serious falling out than he had supposed. Jekyll refers to Lanyon as "that hide-bound pedant . . . an ignorant, blatant pedant." He is angry at Lanyon because Lanyon objects to what he calls Jekyll's "scientific heresies." Jekyll concludes, "I was never more disappointed in any man than Lanyon."

Defeated in his efforts to get to the bottom of the mystery of

Mr. Hyde, Utterson is forced to silence. But a year later an event happens which not only shocks the whole of London by its "singular ferocity" but also reawakens in Utterson his need to get to the bottom of the mystery of the strange relationship between Dr. Jekyll and Mr. Hyde. One late evening, a maid, looking out of her window, sees an old man walking along the street, and, coming the other way, an ugly young man with a cane, whom she recognizes, from a visit he once made to her master, as a certain Mr. Hyde, and for whom she had conceived an instant dislike. When the two met on the street the young man suddenly began to beat the old man unmercifully with the cane, clubbing him to the earth, and trampling him underfoot until the old man's bones were audibly shattered. The maid fainted, and when she awoke the old man was lying there dead on the sidewalk, the murderer long gone, but one half of the cane with which the deed had been done lay there in the gutter—the other, no doubt, having been carried away. The police were summoned, and a purse, gold watch, and letter were found upon the victim's body. The letter bore the name of Mr. Utterson.

The next morning Mr. Utterson was visited by the police, and he was able to identify the old man as his client, the well-known and highly regarded London personality Sir Danvers Carew. When he was told that the maid identified the assailant as one Mr. Hyde he was shocked, but when he was shown the broken cane he turned pale for he recognized the cane as one that he himself gave to his friend, Henry Jekyll, several years before.

Of course Mr. Utterson has Hyde's address, and takes the police to the address in Soho, a dismal quarter of the city. "This was the home of Henry Jekyll's favourite; of a man who was heir to quarter of a million sterling." They knock at the door of the apartment and an evil-faced old woman answers, and grudgingly tells them that this was Mr. Hyde's apartment, but he had left less than an hour ago. The police enter the apartment and find that it was furnished in luxury and in good taste, but that the rooms had obviously been recently ransacked, for clothes are strewn every which way, and there are piles of papers which had been hastily burned. In the debris the police find the butt end of a green cheque book, which had resisted the fire, and the other half of the cane. The police think that now surely they can find the culprit; they need only wait by the bank for him to appear to draw his cash. But the matter does not prove so easy. He had no family, there were no photographs, only a few people had ever seen him, and on only one point could people agree regarding his description: that there was about him a "haunting sense of unexpressed deformity." So Hyde seems for the time being to have effected a complete and total escape.

Mr. Utterson, filled again with anxiety for his friend, goes once more to Jekyll's house where he is admitted by Poole and is led to the doctor's laboratory, the first time he had ever been received in this part of the house. Here he is greeted by his friend, but it is not the ebullient doctor of old, but a Dr. Jekyll who looks deathly sick, who does not rise to meet his visitor, but holds out a cold hand and welcomes him in a changed voice. "You have not been mad enough to hide this fellow?" asks Utterson as the conversation soon centers on the tragic murder and the hunted Hyde. "Utterson," says Jekyll, "I swear to God, I swear to God I will never set eyes on him again. I bind my honour to you that I am done with him in this world. It is all at an end. And indeed he does not want my help; you do not know him as I do; he is safe, he is quite safe; mark my words, he will never more be heard of."

Later in the conversation Utterson offers the thought to Jekyll that Hyde meant to murder him and get the proceeds from the will. "You have had a fine escape," Utterson declares. "I have had what is far more to the purpose," returned the doctor solemnly, "I have had a lesson—O God, Utterson, what a lesson I have had!" And he covered his face for a moment with his hands.

Utterson is somewhat reassured, though he marvels at his

friend's strange behaviour, but before he leaves, Henry Jekyll gives him a letter to read, a letter he had received from Hyde himself which signified briefly that Dr. Jekyll had more than repaid Hyde what he owed to him and that he, Hyde, had a means of escape on which he placed a sure dependence. Jekyll asks Utterson for his advice, and Utterson leaves with the letter to deliberate the matter. But, moved by a strange inspiration, Utterson takes the letter to his friend, Mr. Guest, who is a handwriting expert. By chance a second letter, from Jekyll himself, falls into their hands and Mr. Guest compares the two handwritings. They are, he concludes, from the same hand, differing only in slope, but with a singular resemblance. Utterson is shocked: " 'Henry Jekyll forge for a murderer!' he says to himself. And his blood ran cold in his veins."

So the mystery deepens, and time goes by, and there is no sign of Mr. Hyde. True, news came out of his vile life, of his callousness and violence, and the hatred he received from all who knew him. But he himself has disappeared, and with the disappearance everyone gradually begins to relax. There was also a new life for Henry Jekyll. He came out of seclusion, renewed his friendship with Utterson and Lanyon, became even more dedicated to good works, and "was now no less distinguished for religion" as well.

And so it was for more than two months, until one day Utterson, who had been a daily visitor at his friend's house, found the door at Jekyll's shut against him. "The doctor was confined to the house," Poole the butler told him, "and saw no one." Again and again Utterson was turned away until at last he went to consult Dr. Lanyon about the matter, only to find Lanyon was at death's door. It was not simply his physical deterioration that shook Utterson, it was also "a look in the eye and quality of manner that seemed to testify to some deep-seated terror of the mind." When Utterson brings up the matter of Jekyll, Lanyon bursts into a tirade. "I wish to see or hear no more of Dr. Jekyll!" he exclaims. He can give Utterson no explanation, but only reiterates that nothing can be done and that he wishes to hear no more of "this accursed topic."

Baffled, Utterson returns home and writes to Jekyll inquiring about the unhappy break with Lanyon, and complaining that he has been excluded from the house. He learns in a reply from Jekyll that the quarrel with Lanyon is incurable: "I do not blame our old friend," Jekyll wrote, "but I share his view that we must never meet. I mean from henceforth to lead a life of extreme seclusion; you must not be surprised, nor must you doubt my friendship, if my door is often shut even to you. You must suffer me to go my own dark way. I have brought on myself a punishment and a danger that I cannot name."

Shortly after this Lanyon dies. Greatly affected, Utterson, the night following the funeral, takes from its locked place a letter, carefully sealed, entrusted to him by Lanyon shortly before his death, and inscribed, "Private: for the hands of G.J. Utterson alone, and in the case of his predecease *to be destroyed unread.*"

Reluctantly, Utterson breaks open the seal and, inside, finds another enclosure, marked upon the cover "not to be opened till the death or disappearance of Dr. Henry Jekyll." Here it was again, the allusion to the possible disappearance of Henry Jekyll! Before it had been a notation in Jekyll's will. Now it was inscribed on the inner packet in the handwriting of the dead Dr. Lanyon. Professional ethics restrain Utterson from opening the packet and inspecting its contents and the unread missive is locked away again.

Utterson continues to try to see his friend Jekyll but is consistently turned away and gradually becomes discouraged. Poole tells him that the doctor is now more confined than ever, and that he seldom leaves the laboratory, has grown silent, is out of spirits, and that it seems always as if something is on his mind. Like the master storyteller he is, Stevenson lays out for the reader the many pieces of the puzzle that must all be put together: the mysterious relationship of Jekyll and Hyde, Hyde's almost miraculous disappearance, Jekyll's visible decline and total seclusion after two months of a changed life, Lanyon's inexplicable death, the unexplained break between the two friends, the "forged" letter, the mysterious packet not to be opened until Jekyll's death or disappearance that came to

Utterson via Lanyon before his death, and now Jekyll's unexplainable seclusion.

With no encouragement from Jekyll to renew his vistis, Utterson gradually loses energy to solve the mystery, until one day a shocking incident occurs that sets his mind aflame once again. It happened one Sunday, when Mr. Utterson and Mr. Enfield were on their customary walk, that their way once more took them to the by-street in London where lay the mysterious door that led to Dr. Jekyll's laboratory. Just when the two friends were congratulating themselves that the mysterious matter of Hyde had come to an end, they chanced to see Dr. Jekyll framed in the window of the building like a "disconsolate prisoner." The two friends greeted him with enthusiasm, and for a short while Jekyll returned their warm greetings, almost, so it seemed, accepting their invitation to come down and visit, when "the smile was struck out of his face and succeeded by an expression of such abject terror and despair, as froze the very blood of the two gentlemen below." The window was slammed down, and the two friends below looked at each other with horror in their eyes. "God forgive us, God forgive us," said Mr. Utterson. And silently they walked away.

Shortly after this came the last night. Utterson was seated by his fireside when he had an unexpected visitor: Poole, the butler, who had come because he thought foul play had been done to his master, urges Utterson to accompany him home. Utterson does so, and is greeted with relief by the servants, amongst whom is a frightened housemaid, who breaks into "hysterical whimpering." Taking Utterson to the laboratory door, Poole calls out, "Mr. Utterson, sir, asking to see you." A voice answers from within, "Tell him I cannot see any one," but the voice was not that of Jekyll! Back in the main quarters of the house Poole explains that all week there has been a crying night and day from whoever is in the laboratory for some kind of medicine, and two or three times a day the butler finds written instructions cast outside the laboratory door for Poole to go to this apothecary or that to find a pure version of a drug that is wanted badly, but no matter how many times the prescription is filled it turns out to be unsatisfactory to whoever it is who is in the laboratory waiting in such desperation. And once, Poole relates, he saw the creature himself, as he had slipped out to look for the latest drug brought back from the chemist, the figure of a man with a mask upon his face. "If it was my master," cried out Poole to Utterson, "why did he cry out like a rat, and run from me?" There was someone in the laboratory, someone strange, for "Once," said Poole, "I heard it weeping, weeping like a woman or a lost soul."

Reluctantly the two men conclude that Jekyll has probably been murdered, and that the mysterious intruder can be none other than Edward Hyde; they now feel that they have no choice but to break down the laboratory door. One more time they call out to Jekyll before taking this last desperate move.

"Jekyll," called Utterson, "I demand to see you." But there was no reply. Then: "Utterson!" said a voice, "for God's sake, have mercy!" "Ah, that's not Jekyll's voice—it's Hyde's!" cried Utterson, and with that the two men break down the door.

Suddenly Utterson and Poole stand inside the laboratory. All is still. Then they see the body of a man, still twitching, who has clearly just destroyed himself with poison. It is the body of Edward Hyde, dressed in clothes far too large for him, such as might have fit Dr. Jekyll. They rummage further through the disordered laboratory looking for Jekyll's body, but find nothing. A pious book lies on a table, one known to have been prized by the good doctor, but with startling blasphemies written on the margins. Finally they do locate a laboratory glass, which obviously has been used many times, the sight of which somehow strikes them with horror. At last they come across three envelopes. The first contains a will, drawn up by Henry Jekyll, leaving all his possessions to Gabriel John Utterson. The second is a brief note in the doctor's hand instructing Utterson to read the letter left him by Dr. Lanyon. The third is a "considerable packet sealed in several places." Utterson decides to call the police, but first he reads Dr. Lanyon's letter.

### Dr. Lanyon's Narrative

Four days ago, Lanyon had written to Utterson, he had received a letter from Henry Jekyll, a letter urging him most strongly to postpone all other engagements he might have for tonight, go to Jekyll's house, force open the door to Jekyll's cabinet in his laboratory (Poole having orders to allow Lanyon to do this), and remove all contents and return with them to his home. Then Lanyon is to be alone at midnight in his home and is to admit into his house the person who will present himself in Jekyll's name, and to give this man the contents withdrawn from the cabinet.

Lanyon goes on to relate that he decided to do as he was asked, that he went to Jekyll's laboratory and did remove from the cabinet what appeared to be "a simple crystalline salt of a white colour." At midnight a knock came at his door and Lanyon tells how he found "a small man crouching against the pillars of the portico," a man dressed in clothes outlandishly large for him, who would have been laughable had he not been so revolting. Impatiently the man, who is Hyde, of course, demands the crystalline salts, and "At sight of the contents, he uttered one loud sob of such immense relief that I sat petrified."

The small, revolting man then consumed the drug and began to undergo profound and horrible changes until, there before Lanyon's eyes, stood Henry Jekyll. Lanyon concluded his letter: What he told me in the next hour, I cannot bring my mind to set on paper. I saw what I saw, I heard what I heard, and my soul sickened at it; and yet now when that sight has faded from my eyes, I ask myself if I believe it, and I cannot answer. My life is shaken to its roots; sleep has left me; the deadliest terror sits by me at all hours of the day and night; I feel that my days are numbered, and that I must die; and yet I shall die incredulous." Next the stunned Utterson read the largish packet which proved to be

## Henry Jekyll's Full Statement of the Case

Jekyll's account can be summarized as follows: He began with a description of himself and his life. He was, he writes, born to a large fortune, "fond of the respect of the wise and good among my fellowmen, and thus, as might have been supposed, with every guarantee of an honourable and distinguished future." The worst of his faults, Jekyll noted of himself, "was a certain impatient gaiety of disposition" which seemed harmless enough but which he "found hard to reconcile with my imperious desire to carry my head high, and wear a more than commonly grave countenance before the public." "Hence," he continued, "it came about that I concealed my pleasure; and that when I reached years of reflection, and began to look round me and take stock of my progress and position in the world, I stood already committed to a profound duplicity of life." He goes on to relate how he was guilty of certain irregularities of life which he regarded with a "morbid sense of shame." He had, he noted, a "dual nature," moreover, "both sides of me were in dead earnest; I was no more myself when I laid aside restraint and plunged in shame, than when I laboured, in the eye of day, at the furtherance of knowledge or the relief of sorrow and suffering." From all of this Jekyll concluded, "that man is not truly one, but truly two." He even hazarded the conjecture that man would eventually be "known for a mere policy of multifarious, incongruous, and independent denizens." In this way he came to recognize "the thorough and primitive duality of man."

At this point, Jekyll says, he began to dwell "on the thought of the separation of these elements. If each . . . could but be housed in separate identities, life would be relieved of all that was unbearable." At this point he began to experiment and eventually produced a drug that could accomplish just such a separation of his two personalities, buying from a certain chemist the last special ingredient necessary to make the transformative compound. Jekyll then took the drug and began to undergo profound changes: "I felt younger, lighter, happier in body; within I was conscious of a heady recklessness, a current of disordered sensual images running like a mill race in my fancy, a solution of the bonds of obligation, an unknown but not an innocent freedom of the soul. I knew myself, at the first breath of this new life, to be more wicked, tenfold more wicked, sold a slave to my original evil; and the thought, in that moment, braced and delighted me like wine." He then looked in the mirror and saw that person with whom we have already become familiar: the small, young, somehow deformed body of Edward Hyde.

"This, too," Jekyll reasoned, "was myself." And so Jekyll welcomed Hyde, and concluded, "all human beings . . . are commingled out of good and evil; and Edward Hyde, alone in the ranks of mankind, was pure evil." Now Jekyll found that he had but to quaff the drug and he was transformed into Hyde, and could then indulge in all those pleasures which hitherto he either had forbade himself, or had indulged in only with guilt and anxiety that he might be discovered. To make it even easier, he took the apartment in Soho where, as Hyde, he could live as he pleased, and he also drew up the will to which Utterson had so greatly objected. At first the pleasures he pursued were simply "undignified," but, in Hyde's hands, they soon began to "turn towards the monstrous." But Jekyll felt no guilt, for it "was Hyde, after all, and Hyde alone that was guilty. Jekyll was no worse; he woke again to his good qualities seemingly unimpaired; he would even make haste, where it was possible, to undo the evil done by Hyde. And thus conscience slumbered."

So everything proceeded for a while as Jekyll had planned until one dark day he found that he had turned into Hyde even without taking the drug! "Yes, I had gone to bed Henry Jekyll; I had awakened Edward Hyde." Jekyll was terrified. How could he return to his normal shape and personality? He found the answer by taking the drug, which this time reversed him from Hyde to Jekyll again.

Because of this frightening experience Jekyll felt he now had to choose between his two personalities. It was a hard choice, but at last he determined to remain as Jekyll, though he did not give up the house in Soho, nor destroy the clothes of Edward Hyde which he kept in his cabinet. For two months he led a life of great severity, until at length he "began to be tortured with throes and longings, as of Hyde struggling after freedom; and at last, in an hour of moral weakness, I once again compounded and swallowed the transforming draught."

It was at this time that Hyde killed Dr. Carew. "Instantly the spirit of hell awoke in me and raged. With a transport of glee, I mauled the unresisting body, tasting delight from every blow; and it was not till weariness had begun to succeed, that I was suddenly, in the top fit of my delirium, struck through the heart by a cold thrill of terror." Then, when Hyde took the draught, and his usual personality reemerged, Jekyll wrote that "Henry Jekyll, with streaming tears of gratitude and remorse, had fallen upon his knees and lifted his clasped hands to God."

Henceforth, Jekyll realized, he could no longer be Hyde, for Hyde was now a wanted man. He now must confine himself to "the better part of my existence." So Jekyll once again lived a life dedicated to the good, until one day, as he sat in the park reflecting that he was, after all, "like my neighbors; . . . comparing myself with other men, comparing my active good-will with the lazy cruelty of their neglect," he suddenly was transformed into Hyde! Now his situation was desperate. He must not be seen in public, yet if he returned home in the form of Hyde his own servants would turn him in. It was at this point that he wote the letter to Lanyon, and with the doctor's help, recovered the drug and became again his Jekyll self.

Jekyll now lived in horror of his other self but found that he could not avoid unwilling transformations into Hyde even without the drug. So he was consigned to a life of confinement in his laboratory where he could get at the drug when this happened, but he also discovered that more and more of the drug was required to bring him from the form of Hyde back into the form of Jekyll. "The powers of Hyde," he noted, "seemed to have grown with the sickliness of Jekyll." And then—he began to run out of the drug!

He was now, of course, confined to the laboratory, and slipped frequently into the form of Edward Hyde. It was in this form that Poole once saw him outside the laboratory door with his face masked. Desperately he sent Poole out repeatedly to ransack London for the correct ingredient with which to make a new supply of the drug, but always it failed to work. Only gradually did he realize that "my first supply was impure, and that it was that unknown impurity which lent efficacy to the draught." Jekyll concluded his letter (and with this Stevenson also concludes the story):

About a week has passed, and I am now finishing this statement under the influence of the last of the old powders. This, then, is the last time, short of a miracle, that Henry Jekyll can think his own thoughts or see his own face (now how sadly altered!) in the glass. Nor must I delay too long to bring my writing to an end; for if my narrative has hitherto escaped destruction, it has been by a combination of great prudence and great good luck. Should the throes of change take me in the act of writing it, Hyde will tear it in pieces; but if some time shall have elapsed after I have laid it by, his wonderful selfishness and circumscription to the moment will probably save it once again from the action of his apelike spite. And indeed the doom that is closing on us both has already changed and crushed him. Half an hour from now, when I shall again and forever reindue that hated personality, I know how I shall sit shuddering and weeping in my chair, or continue, with the most strained and fearstruck ecstasy of listening, to pace up and down this room (my last earthly refuge) and give ear to every sound of menace. Will Hyde die upon the scaffold? or will he find courage to release himself at the last moment? God knows; I am careless; this is my true hour of death, and what is to follow concerns another than myself. Here then, as I lay down the pen and proceed to seal up my confession, I bring the life of that unhappy Henry Jekyll to an end.

# Subject Index

# Scripture Index